ATMOSPHERE

Air Pollution and Its Effects

OUR FRAGILE PLANET

Atmosphere

Biosphere

Climate

Geosphere

Humans and the Natural Environment

Hydrosphere

Oceans

Polar Regions

ATMOSPHERE

Air Pollution and Its Effects

DANA DESONIE, PH.D.

CHELSEA HOUSE
PUBLISHERS

An imprint of Infobase Publishing

Atmosphere

Copyright © 2007 by Dana Desonie, Ph.D.

Chelsea House
An imprint of Infobase Publishing
132 West 31st Street
New York NY 10001

Library of Congress Cataloging-in-Publication Data
Desonie, Dana.
   Atmosphere / Dana Desonie.
     p. cm. — (Our fragile planet)
   Includes bibliographical references and index.
   ISBN-13: 978-0-8160-6213-3 (hardcover)
   ISBN-10: 0-8160-6213-7 (hardcover)
   1. Atmosphere. 2. Weather. 3. Meteorology. I. Title. II. Series.
   QC861.3.D47 2007
   551.5--dc22   2007008241

Chelsea House books are available at special discounts when purchased in bulk quantities for businesses, associations, institutions, or sales promotions. Please call our Special Sales Department in New York at (212) 967-8800 or (800) 322-8755.

You can find Chelsea House on the World Wide Web at http://www.chelseahouse.com

Text design by Annie O'Donnell
Cover design by Ben Peterson

Cover Photograph: © Jerome Scholler/Shutterstock.com

Printed in the United States of America

Bang FOF 10 9 8 7 6 5 4 3 2 1

This book is printed on acid-free paper.

All links and Web addresses were checked and verified to be correct at the time of publication. Because of the dynamic nature of the Web, some addresses and links may have changed since publication and may no longer be valid.

Contents

Preface   vii

Acknowledgments   ix

Introduction   x

⊕ PART ONE:
What the Atmosphere Provides   1

1. The Gases and What They Do   3

2. The Atmosphere: Past and Present   13

3. The Motions of the Atmosphere   22

4. Other Factors That Shape a Region's Climate   35

⊕ PART TWO:
Atmospheric Behavior: The Weather   43

5. What Makes the Weather?   45

6. Extreme Weather   59

⊕ PART THREE:
Human Influence on the Atmosphere:
Local Impacts   79

7. Air Pollutants and Air Pollution   81

8. Air Pollution and the Environment   92

9. Air Pollution and Human Health   101

10. Acid Rain   110

11. Air Pollution Control   123

12. The Atmosphere Above Cities   138

⊕ **PART FOUR:**
Human Influence on the Atmosphere:
Global Impacts   **145**

13. Ozone Loss in the Stratosphere   147

14. Climate Change   157

Conclusion   169

Glossary   173

Further Reading   183

Index   189

Preface

The planet is a marvelous place: a place with blue skies, wild storms, deep lakes, and rich and diverse ecosystems. The tides ebb and flow, baby animals are born in the spring, and tropical rain forests harbor an astonishing array of life. The Earth sustains living things and provides humans with the resources to maintain a bountiful way of life: water, soil, and nutrients to grow food, and the mineral and energy resources to build and fuel modern society, among many other things.

The physical and biological sciences provide an understanding of the whys and hows of natural phenomena and processes—why the sky is blue and how metals form, for example—and insights into how the many parts are interrelated. Climate is a good example. Among the many influences on the Earth's climate are the circulation patterns of the atmosphere and the oceans, the abundance of plant life, the quantity of various gases in the atmosphere, and even the sizes and shapes of the continents. Clearly, to understand climate it is necessary to have a basic understanding of several scientific fields and to be aware of how these fields are interconnected.

As Earth scientists like to say, the only thing constant about our planet is change. From the ball of dust, gas, and rocks that came together 4.6 billion years ago to the lively and diverse globe that orbits the Sun today, very little about the Earth has remained the same for long. Yet, while change is fundamental, people have altered the environment unlike any other species in Earth's history. Everywhere there are reminders of our presence. A look at the sky might show a sooty cloud or a jet contrail. A look at the sea might reveal plastic refuse, oil, or only a few fish swimming where once they had been countless. The land has been deforested and strip-mined. Rivers and lakes have been polluted. Changing conditions and habitats have caused some plants and animals to expand their populations, while others have become extinct. Even the climate—which for millennia was thought to be beyond human influence—has been shifting due to alterations in the makeup of atmospheric gases brought about by human activities. The planet is changing fast and people are the primary cause.

OUR FRAGILE PLANET is a set of eight books that celebrate the wonders of the world by highlighting the scientific processes behind them. The books also look at the science underlying the tremendous influence humans are having on the environment. The set is divided into volumes based on the large domains on which humans have had an impact: *Atmosphere, Climate, Hydrosphere, Oceans, Geosphere, Biosphere,* and *Polar Regions.* The volume *Humans and the Natural Environment* describes the impact of human activity on the planet and explores ways in which we can live more sustainably.

A core belief expressed in each volume is that to mitigate the impacts humans are having on the Earth, each of us must understand the scientific processes that operate in the natural world. We must understand how human activities disrupt those processes and use that knowledge to predict ways that changes in one system will affect seemingly unrelated systems. These books express the belief that science is the solid ground from which we can reach an agreement on the behavioral changes that we must adopt—both as individuals and as a society—to solve the problems caused by the impact of humans on our fragile planet.

Acknowledgments

I would like to thank, above all, the scientists who have dedicated their lives to the study of the Earth, especially those engaged in the important work of understanding how human activities are impacting the planet. Many thanks to the staff of Facts On File and Chelsea House for their guidance and editing expertise: Frank Darmstadt, Executive Editor; Brian Belval, Senior Editor; and Leigh Ann Cobb, independent developmental editor. Dr. Tobi Zausner located the color images that illustrate our planet's incredible beauty and the harsh reality of the effects human activities are having on it. Thanks also to my agent, Jodie Rhodes, who got me involved in this project.

Family and friends were a great source of support and encouragement as I wrote these books. Special thanks to the May '97 Moms, who provided the virtual water cooler that kept me sane during long days of writing. Cathy Propper was always enthusiastic as I was writing the books, and even more so when they were completed. My mother, Irene Desonie, took great care of me as I wrote for much of June 2006. Mostly importantly, my husband, Miles Orchinik, kept things moving at home when I needed extra writing time and provided love, support, and encouragement when I needed that, too. This book is dedicated to our children, Reed and Maya, who were always loving, and usually patient. I hope these books do a small bit to help people understand how their actions impact the future for all children.

Introduction

Without its atmosphere—the envelope of gases that surrounds a planet or moon—the Earth would be unrecognizable. With no gases for light or sound to travel through, the skies would be black and silent. With no air in which to float or fly, pollen, birds, and airplanes would fall to the ground. Of course, there would be no plants, animals, or airplanes, since there would be no gaseous molecules to support life or to protect organisms from the Sun's harmful, high-energy radiation. The planet would be uninhabitable, except perhaps for the simplest life forms. As on the Moon, temperatures would be scorching in the day and frigid at night, and the temperature difference between the equator and the poles would be extreme. There would be no weather—clouds could not form and rain would not fall—and, by extension, there would be no climate. It would be a very different world: a world more like Mars than the Earth.

Fortunately, the Earth does have an atmosphere, even though it is very thin when compared to the size of the planet. Its gases provide some of the raw ingredients necessary for the manufacture of food by plants and for the use of food energy by living things. Ozone gas clustered in a layer of the upper atmosphere protects the planet's life by filtering out the incoming radiation of the Sun's most harmful rays. Greenhouse gases store heat, resulting in global temperatures that are much more moderate than they otherwise would be.

The atmosphere is the location of all weather, whether it is a mild summer breeze or a devastating hurricane. The weather may bring much-needed rain or an unremitting drought. Winds serve the planet by delivering heat from warmer regions to cooler ones, resulting in a more evenly heated globe. Rains convey moisture from wet regions—especially from the oceans—to drier areas, allowing them to be inhabited by plants and animals. A region's climate is the long-term average pattern of its weather, which is shaped by its latitude, its position in atmospheric circulation patterns, and its proximity to oceans and mountain ranges, among other features.

The atmosphere is useful to humans for more than just these natural processes. People exploit the atmosphere's vastness by using it as a repository for the gaseous waste products of industrial society. And now the quantity of air pollution is overtaking us. Cities, rural areas, and even national parks are plagued by polluted air. Pollutants created by the burning of fuels or forests or by the manufacture of chemicals rise into the air above an area, resulting in reduced visibility, an altered environment, and compromised

Earth's atmosphere is an extremely thin layer compared to the size of the planet. *(NASA)*

human health. Some pollutants combine with water in the atmosphere to create acids that fall as rain. This acid rain degrades forests, freshwater environments, and cultural objects. Even heat can be a pollutant. Some urban areas have experienced temperature increases in recent decades due to waste heat from modern machinery and the way that concrete and other manmade surfaces intensify the effects of solar radiation. Programs to reduce pollution have been very successful with some pollutants in some areas, although as populations and machinery increase, there is always more that needs to be done.

Air pollutants do not just harm the local or regional environment; they also can cause damage on a global scale. Certain man-made chemicals have damaged the planet's protective ozone layer, allowing more harmful solar radiation to strike the Earth's surface. Although the use of these chemicals is being phased out, their destructive effects will linger for many more decades. Rising concentrations of greenhouse gases, the result of human activities like fossil fuel burning, have boosted global temperatures. This has already brought about a rise in sea level, more extreme weather, and melting glaciers and ice caps. Many more alterations to the environment are inevitable as temperatures continue to climb. Efforts to reduce greenhouse gas emissions have had only limited success thus far, but the world is becoming increasingly aware of the need to find solutions.

Part One of *Atmosphere* describes the function of the atmosphere and discusses interesting phenomena such as the cause of rainbows. Part Two looks at the weather, both normal and extreme, and shows why even the most extreme weather is normal for some locations. Air pollutants and their effect on the environment and human health are covered in Part Three. Pollutants that cause global damage, either by destroying the ozone layer or by causing global warming, are discussed in Part Four.

PART ONE

WHAT THE ATMOSPHERE PROVIDES

The Gases and
What They Do

This chapter describes the gases that comprise the Earth's **atmosphere** and their functions. An atmosphere is the gases and particles that surround a planet or a moon. Some of the Earth's atmospheric gases, like oxygen and carbon dioxide, are essential for plants and animals as they carry out life processes. A few gases trap heat and keep the planet's temperatures moderate. One particular gas protects Earth's life from the Sun's harmful radiation. Human activities, such as the burning of gasoline in cars, have added **pollutants** to the atmosphere. Air pollutants are substances that are found in unnatural quantities in the atmosphere or in a region of the atmosphere where they do not belong, or that are made by humans and do not belong in the atmosphere at all.

THE GASES NEEDED FOR BIOLOGICAL PROCESSES

Nitrogen (N_2) and oxygen (O_2) make up 99% of the gases found in the atmosphere. Although other components comprise only the remaining

Concentrations of Atmospheric Gases

GAS	SYMBOL	CONCENTRATION (%)
Nitrogen	N_2	78.08
Oxygen	O_2	20.95
Argon	Ar	0.93
Neon	Ne	0.0018
Helium	He	0.0005
Hydrogen	H	0.00006
Xenon	Xe	0.000009
Water vapor	H_2O	0 to 4
Carbon dioxide	CO_2	0.036
Methane	CH_4	0.00017
Nitrous oxide	N_2O	0.00003
Ozone	O_3	0.000004
Particles (dust, soot)		0.000001
Chlorofluorocarbons (CFCs)		0.00000002

1%, some are extremely important. The table above is a list of atmospheric gases and their concentrations.

Many gases are in balance in the atmosphere; that is, the amount that enters, the **input**, equals the amount that leaves, the **output**. Nitrogen, the most abundant atmospheric gas, is in balance. This gas is input by the decay of plants and animals and is output by the activities of bacteria in the soil. Argon, neon, helium, and xenon—the **noble gases**—are also in balance. These gases are colorless, odorless, tasteless and chemically **inert**; they do not undergo chemical reactions with other elements or compounds.

Carbon dioxide (CO_2) and oxygen (O_2) are the most important gases for living organisms. CO_2 is a tiny component of the atmosphere, accounting for only 36 out of every 100,000 gas molecules, yet it is fundamental to nearly all life on Earth. The gas is essential for **photosynthesis**, the process by which plants take raw materials that are abundant in the environment and turn them into food. In photosynthesis, plants use CO_2 and water (H_2O) to produce sugar ($C_6H_{12}O_6$) and oxygen (O_2). The simplified chemical reaction for photosynthesis is:

$$6CO_2 + 12H_2O + \text{solar energy} = C_6H_{12}O_6 + 6O_2 + 6H_2O$$

The sugar and oxygen produced by photosynthesis are then available for **respiration**. This process uses oxygen to convert sugar into energy that plants and animals can use. The chemical equation for respiration looks like photosynthesis in reverse:

$$C_6H_{12}O_6 + 6O_2 = 6CO_2 + 6H_2O + \text{energy}$$

Respiration and photosynthesis are gas exchange processes: In photosynthesis, CO_2 is converted to O_2, and in respiration, O_2 is converted to CO_2.

Carbon dioxide is absorbed from the atmosphere in several ways. Most importantly, CO_2 is used by plants during photosynthesis. CO_2 is also stored in plant tissue and in soil, where it goes when plants decay. In the oceans, CO_2 moves freely between the sea surface and the atmosphere, but when it sinks into the deep sea, the gas is sequestered from the atmosphere. CO_2 gas also enters the atmosphere by respiration, during volcanic eruptions, and when plant materials decay or burn.

The CO_2 content of the atmosphere is currently not in balance. Although the inputs and outputs from respiration and photosynthesis are equal, humans are increasing the input of CO_2 by burning plants for agricultural purposes and by burning **fossil fuels**, which are made

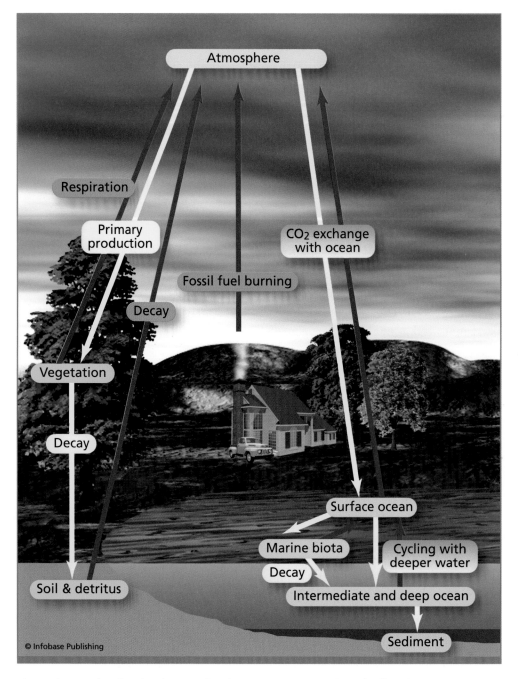

The carbon cycle, showing inputs of carbon into the atmosphere (red) and outputs of carbon from the atmosphere (yellow).

from ancient plants that the Earth's processes have transformed into oil, gas, or coal for use by humans as fuel. The effects of rising levels of CO_2 in the atmosphere are the topic of Chapter 14.

Oxygen as O_2 is in balance in the atmosphere, and its levels do not change with time. Photosynthesis is the major input of this gas and respiration is the major output.

OZONE FOR PROTECTION FROM ULTRAVIOLET RADIATION

Ozone is a molecule composed of three oxygen atoms (O_3). In the layer of the upper atmosphere known as the **stratosphere**, ozone filters out the Sun's harmful high-energy **ultraviolet (UV) radiation**. The ozone molecule forms in the stratosphere when UV energy breaks down some O_2 molecules to make single O-atoms. These O-atoms then bond with other O_2 molecules to form O_3. The reverse process also takes place in the stratosphere as UV energy breaks apart O_3 molecules to make O_2 and O. The breaking down of O_3 into O_2 and O absorbs the most dangerous UV radiation, UVC, which comes in from the Sun.

By filtering out UVC, stratospheric ozone protects living things at or near the Earth's surface. Stratospheric ozone is concentrated in what is called the **ozone layer**, where the high-energy UV is broken down. Normally, inputs and outputs of O_3 into the ozone layer are equal, but in recent decades, human activities have brought about a decrease in stratospheric ozone. The cause and effects of ozone depletion are discussed in Chapter 13.

A RESERVOIR FOR WATER

To keep water moving between the atmosphere and the Earth's surface, the gaseous form of water, or **water vapor**, must pass through the atmosphere. While air is never dry, the amount of water vapor it contains varies from place to place and from time to time. This fact is obvious when comparing a summer day in Atlanta, Georgia, with a winter night in Fairbanks, Alaska. **Humidity** is the concentration of water vapor in the air. Up to 4% of the volume of the air can be water vapor. This vapor is created in the atmosphere when liquid water at the Earth's surface changes from a liquid to a gas, a process called **evapo-**

Radiation

Radiation is the emission and transmission of energy through space or through solid, liquid, or gaseous material. This could include sound waves passing through water, heat spreading out in a sheet of metal, or light traveling through air. Every object—for example, a human body, this book, the Sun—radiates energy since it contains billions of rapidly vibrating electrons. The energy travels outward as waves, which are called **electromagnetic waves** since they have electrical and magnetic properties.

Waves occur in different lengths, depending on their energy. One **wavelength** is the distance from crest to crest (or trough to trough). All types of radiation, no matter what their wavelength, travel at the speed of light. The wavelengths of energy that an object emits depend primarily on the object's temperature: The higher its temperature, the faster its electrons vibrate, and the shorter the wavelengths of radiation it emits. In materials at high temperature, the molecules smash together rapidly and generate heat. When that material cools

down, the molecules move more slowly. They smash together less frequently and so generate less heat.

Heat is a measure of the total energy of an object; it is the average energy of every molecule multiplied by the total number of molecules. So while a candle flame has higher temperature, a bathtub of hot water contains more heat because it contains more molecules. Heat is measured in calories, an older metric unit; British thermal units (Btu), an English unit; or sometimes in joules, a measure that is used for all forms of energy.

The Sun emits radiation at all wavelengths but nearly half (44%) is in the part of the electromagnetic spectrum known as visible light. These are the only wavelengths to which the human eye is sensitive. When all wavelengths of visible light are together, the light appears white. When they are separated into a spectrum, each wavelength corresponds to a different color. From the longest to the shortest wavelengths, visible light is broken into the colors red, orange, yellow, green, blue, and violet. Wavelengths shorter than vio-

ration. Although water vapor is invisible, it may convert into tiny liquid droplets, in a process known as **condensation**, to form clouds. The droplets can come together to create **precipitation**—rain, sleet, hail, snow, frost, or dew.

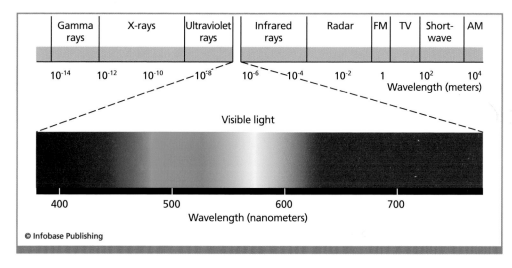

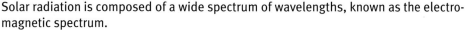

Solar radiation is composed of a wide spectrum of wavelengths, known as the electromagnetic spectrum.

let are called ultraviolet, and wavelengths longer than red are called **infrared**.

Due to the Sun's high temperature, about 7% of what it emits is shortwave, or ultraviolet, radiation. Since short waves carry more energy than long waves, ultraviolet waves carry more energy than visible light waves. Ultraviolet radiation comes in three types: UVA, UVB, and UVC. The last has the shortest wavelength and so is the most dangerous, followed by UVB, then UVA. Infrared energy is also known as heat. Microwaves, TV waves, short radio waves, and AM radio waves have wavelengths beyond the infrared. The Earth's surface absorbs sunlight in the visible and ultraviolet light wavelengths and then reemits the energy in the infrared as heat. This energy is not visible, although it can be picked up by infrared sensors.

GREENHOUSE GASES FOR INSULATION

Carbon dioxide and several other gases, both natural and man-made, are **greenhouse gases**. The presence of greenhouse gases makes complex life on the Earth possible. Although UVC and some UVB are filtered out by the ozone layer, most of the Sun's radiation (lower energy UV and visible light) passes through the atmosphere unimpeded. When this radiation hits the planet's surface, the energy is absorbed by soil, rock, concrete, or water and then is reemitted as heat.

Greenhouse gases in the atmosphere trap some of this heat and cause the atmosphere to warm, a property known as **insulation**. The warming of the atmosphere is called the **greenhouse effect** because it works somewhat like the glass on a greenhouse. Without the greenhouse effect, the Earth's average atmospheric temperature would be a very low 0°F (-18°C). Temperatures also would be extremely variable, scorching in the daytime and frigid at night, such as those on the Moon and the planets that have no atmosphere.

Most greenhouse gases are present naturally in the environment. For example, carbon dioxide is input by respiration, volcanic eruptions, and the burning of plant material. Another greenhouse gas, **methane**, is a hydrocarbon gas (an organic compound composed of hydrogen and carbon) with a variety of inputs including the breakdown of plant material by bacteria in rice paddies and the biochemical reactions that occur in cow stomachs (i.e., by cows passing gas). The **nitrous oxides**, NO and NO_2—referred to together as NO_x—are produced naturally by bacteria. Ozone is found naturally in the lower atmosphere in small amounts. Some man-made gases, such as **chlorofluorocarbons** (**CFCs**), are not present naturally and are greenhouse gases in the lower atmosphere.

PARTICULATES FOR CONDENSATION

Solid and liquid particles in the atmosphere, called **particulates** or **aerosols**, are necessary for the development of clouds and precipitation. Particulates provide a nucleus for water vapor to condense on to form clouds and precipitates such as raindrops and snowflakes. Particulates are solid particles that are light enough to stay suspended in the air and include windblown dust and soil, fecal matter, metal beads, saltwater droplets, smoke from fires, and volcanic ash. Some particulates are the result of human activities, such as fossil fuel burning.

A SINK FOR WASTES

The atmosphere provides a place for the gaseous waste products of modern human society to go. For this reason, it contains gases that were never before in the atmosphere, such as CFCs, or that are present in unnatural locations or quantities. **Air pollution** has a variety of effects, from raising global temperature, to destroying natural atmospheric processes, to simply dirtying the air.

Fossil fuel burning releases enormous quantities of pollutants, including nitrogen dioxide (NO_2), sulfur dioxide (SO_2), carbon monoxide (CO), and hydrocarbons. Some pollutants do not come directly from fossil fuel emissions but are the result of secondary chemical reactions. For example, the action of sunlight on nitrogen oxide and hydrocarbon pollutants in the lower atmosphere forms ozone (O_3). While ozone in the stratosphere is beneficial, in the lower atmosphere—the **troposphere**—this gas is a pollutant and is the primary component of **photochemical smog**, which is air pollution that results from a chemical reaction involving pollutants and sunlight. Also known as "bad" ozone, it can be extremely harmful to animals, plants, and humans. It is also a greenhouse gas.

While atmospheric greenhouse gases are inarguably good for the planet and its life, increased levels of greenhouse gases are not. Additional greenhouse gases amplify the insulating properties of the atmosphere and result in a boost in global temperatures. Increased atmospheric greenhouse gases are responsible for at least some of the current warming of the planet. Of the greenhouse gases that are increasing, carbon dioxide is not the most potent, but it is the one that is most on the rise. Plants store CO_2 in their tissues, and plant materials that have been converted to fossil fuels emit CO_2 when burned. As a result, atmospheric CO_2 levels have been rising sharply since the

Industrial Revolution began about 150 years ago. Methane levels have been going up for the past century due to the expanded agricultural production necessitated by the swelling human population. Water vapor levels are increasing because warm air holds more water vapor than cool air.

Chlorofluorocarbons (CFCs) are greenhouse gases that are released into the lower atmosphere and destroy the ozone layer when they reach the upper atmosphere. These man-made chemicals were once widely used. Production of them peaked in 1986, and they are now being phased out. These compounds are extremely stable and they continue to be present in the atmosphere.

WRAP-UP

Atmospheric gases support life by assisting with the production (photosynthesis) and utilization (respiration) of food energy, by protecting life on Earth from harmful solar rays (the ozone layer), by keeping global air temperatures moderate (the greenhouse effect), and by providing a reservoir for water by forming clouds and precipitation. Besides providing life support, the atmosphere gives humans a sink for gaseous pollutants.

The Atmosphere: Past and Present

Earth's atmosphere formed from physical and biological processes that took place over billions of years. Although the atmosphere is a continuous cloak of gas molecules and other particles, this cloak can be divided into layers, or strata. These strata are not based on the composition of the atmosphere itself, because the types of gases and their abundance relative to each other do not vary much. (The one extremely important exception to this is the stratospheric ozone layer, which protects the planet from the Sun's most harmful rays.)

Primarily, the atmosphere is divided into layers based on how the air temperature decreases with height in the lower atmosphere and increases with height in the upper atmosphere. The **density** (mass per unit volume) of gases decreases with the increase in height above mean sea level, as well. Nearly the entire atmosphere of the Earth—99%—lies within 19 miles (30 kilometers) of sea level. At around 435 miles (700 km) out, the atmosphere is almost completely devoid of matter.

THE EVOLUTION OF THE ATMOSPHERE

The Earth formed from a swirling cloud of dust and gas about 4.5 billion years ago. Gases entered the atmosphere from two main sources: inner space and outer space. Gases that were trapped in the Earth's interior were part of its inner space. Just as they do today, gases—about 80% water (H_2O), 10% carbon dioxide (CO_2), and a few percent nitrogen (N)—erupted from volcanoes and steam vents. From outer space came comets that were composed of ices and trapped gases—primarily H_2O, CO, CO_2, methane, and ammonia, along with some organic compounds. These gases were liberated as the comets struck the planet.

These gases, from both inner and outer space, formed the planet's early atmosphere. Water vapor condensed, formed clouds, and precipitated, leading to the creation of rivers, lakes, and oceans on the barren surface. The early ocean absorbed CO_2, yet the gas was still many times more abundant in the atmosphere than it is today. Thus, the greenhouse effect was much stronger at that time. The planet was not hotter than it is now because the Sun did not burn as brightly. Under these early Earth conditions, surface water was stable as a liquid, a necessity for the origin of life.

As now, nitrogen was the most abundant gas, but the second most abundant gas today, oxygen (O_2), was barely present. This is because there were no plants, and, without them, there was no photosynthesis, which is the source of nearly all of the planet's oxygen. Without oxygen, there was no protective ozone layer, and life could not evolve beyond very simple, single-celled organisms. Once single-celled plants evolved and colonized the planet, they supplied O_2 to the atmosphere.

For hundreds of millions of years, O_2 was taken up by the many elements and compounds that were waiting to combine with oxygen, a process called **oxidation**. (Iron will readily oxidize to rust when oxygen is available, for example.) Only after the exposed minerals were oxidized could O_2 build up in the atmosphere, and only then could animals arise. Once multi-cellular plants were able to survive, between 1 billion and 543 million years ago, they added oxygen to the atmosphere rapidly. At about 450 million years ago, the planet reached its present oxygen level of 21%.

With the proliferation of complex life forms, the composition of the atmosphere became fairly stable. Quantities of nitrogen and oxygen and most other gases have remained about the same for hundreds of millions of years. Carbon dioxide levels have always been variable, depending on input from volcanic eruptions and input or output into the oceans and plant materials. Water vapor is variable, depending on local conditions.

There is a synergy between the Earth's atmosphere and its organisms. It is no accident that plants and animals live in an atmosphere that is mutually favorable to them. Organisms evolve

A World Without an Atmosphere

If Earth had never developed an atmosphere, the planet would be cold, dark, and soundless. Atmospheric gases are also necessary for the transmission of sound waves. It might be a shock to viewers of science-fiction television shows and movies, but sounds cannot be heard in a vacuum. An explosion in outer space would be seen but not heard! Sound waves must have a medium to travel through—a medium that can move back and forth, such as air, ground, or water. As the sound wave moves through the medium, the medium compresses and then rebounds to its normal state after the wave has passed. The wave then compresses the region adjacent to the medium—this is how the sound wave travels. The speed of sound in the atmosphere depends on the density of the air through which it is traveling. The speed of sound is faster in humid air than it is in dry air and is faster in water than it is in the atmosphere.

A world without an atmosphere would be a world without flight. Like sound, birds, insects, and airplanes must have a medium to travel through. They can glide only because the air pressure above their wings is lower than the air pressure beneath. The difference in pressure is known as lift. Lift acts roughly perpendicular to the wing surface and keeps the flyer from falling. By flapping their wings, birds can move in a forward direction and can increase their speed. Without air to hold it up and to push against, no animal or human-built aircraft would be able to fly.

to live in the environment that is available. What is important in biological **evolution** is adapting to, and staying adapted to, the environment. But, in very important ways, the composition of the Earth's atmosphere has also been shaped by the organisms that live in it. With their intertwined cycles of photosynthesis and respiration, plants and animals have kept O_2 and CO_2 at favorable levels for themselves for hundreds of millions of years. Not only have they adapted to their environment, but they also have worked together to create it.

By adding CO_2 and other greenhouse gases to the atmosphere, modern human society has disturbed the long-term balance of the atmospheric gases. Chemicals that have never existed in nature, such as chlorofluorocarbons (CFCs), have been introduced into the atmosphere. Ozone is being added to the lower atmosphere, where it does harm by helping to create smog, and depleted from the upper atmosphere, where it does good by protecting the Earth from the dangerous forms of UV radiation.

ATMOSPHERIC PRESSURE AND TEMPERATURE

Air is made of gas molecules that can move freely. Like all matter, air molecules are attracted to the Earth by its gravity, which draws objects to the center of the planet. Gravity is strongest at lower **altitude** (the height above sea level) and air molecules are packed closest together at sea level. Air is also compressed by the weight of all the air above it. The weight of a column of air from the top of the atmosphere onto a person's shoulders at sea level is more than one ton. But people and animals are not crushed because billions of molecules inside our bodies are pushing outward to compensate. The force of the air weighing down over a unit of area is known as its **atmospheric pressure**, or air pressure.

Atmospheric pressure decreases with increasing altitude because there is less gravity and less air to weigh down from above. Air density, then, is greatest at the Earth's surface and decreases with altitude.

Each 3.7-mile (6-km) increase in altitude reduces the weight of the atmosphere above it by half so that at 18,000 feet (5,500 meters) above sea level, air pressure is only half of what it is at sea level. People feel changes in atmospheric pressure while on an airplane or driving through the mountains when their ears "pop" as they go up or down in altitude. This occurs because the air molecules inside their ears maintain the density of the previous altitude until they have had a chance to equilibrate with the air pressure at the new altitude.

The dense packing of air molecules near the Earth's surface restricts the ability of each molecule to move. At sea level, a molecule can travel an average distance of less than one millionth of a centimeter before it collides with another molecule. Each collision between molecules releases heat, so the air at sea level is relatively warm. At higher altitudes, where the molecules are not packed in so tightly, they are less likely to collide, so the air becomes cooler.

The transfer of heat is important for driving the motions of the atmosphere. Heat transfer occurs in two different ways. **Conduction** is the transfer of heat through a substance that has different temperatures in different parts. Because warm atoms and molecules move more vigorously than cold ones, the particles in the warmer region strike their neighbors, transferring heat until it is evenly distributed. **Convection** transfers heat by the movement of currents. Think of a room with a floor heater. As the air near the heater becomes warmer, the air's density decreases and it rises. The air near the ceiling is pushed sideways by the rising air. The sideways movement of air is called **advection**. Because the air pushed along the ceiling is now far from the heater, it is relatively cool. When it becomes denser than the air beneath it, it sinks. The air then moves by advection along the ground until it again is near the heater. The circuit described above is a **convection cell**. Warm air rises to make a **low pressure zone**, cool air sinks to make a **high pressure zone**, and air moves between the two.

Something else happens to air as it rises or sinks. Warm air can hold more moisture than cold air, so as warm air rises and cools, it is able to hold less moisture, which may result in precipitation. On

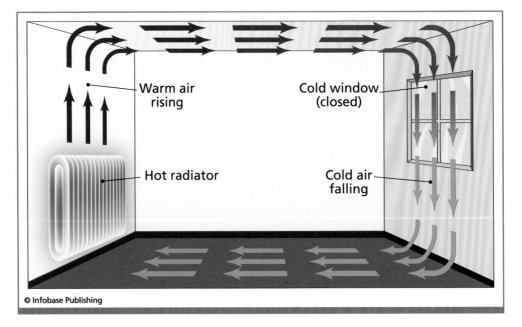

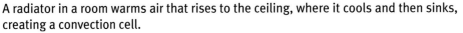

A radiator in a room warms air that rises to the ceiling, where it cools and then sinks, creating a convection cell.

the other hand, sinking air becomes warmer and therefore can hold more water, which may result in evaporation of water from the Earth's surface.

THE LAYERS OF THE ATMOSPHERE

The composition of atmospheric gases is about the same at different altitudes, with the important exception of the ozone layer. Despite being similar in its composition throughout, the atmosphere is divided into layers that are defined primarily by **temperature gradient**, which is the change of temperature that occurs with distance (or, in this case, altitude).

The layer nearest the Earth's surface, rising from sea level to about 6 miles (11 km), is the troposphere. The primary heat source for the troposphere is infrared energy (heat) that radiates from Earth's surface. This layer measures a decrease in temperature of about 3.6°F per

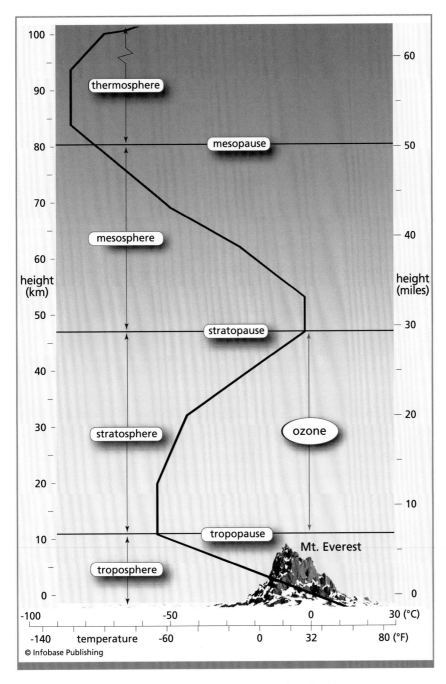

The layers of the atmosphere are defined by whether they increase or decrease in temperature with altitude, except the ozone layer, which is named for its relatively large concentration of ozone molecules.

1,000 feet (6.5°C per 1,000 m) of altitude. The value fluctuates with the day, the location, and the season. Sometimes a portion of the troposphere has a **temperature inversion** and the situation is reversed: Air temperature increases with height. Almost all of the weather found at the planet's surface is due to the vertical movement of air in the troposphere.

The stratosphere rises from the top of the troposphere to about 30 miles (45 km). Since this layer is heated by the Sun's UV rays, it gets warmer with increasing proximity to the Sun. The warm air of the upper stratosphere "floats" on the cooler air of the lower stratosphere, since it is less dense. With warmer air above cooler air, the stratosphere is very stable vertically. This layer usually experiences very little turbulence, which is why commercial airliners fly at this level. Not only does air within the stratosphere not mix, but also there is almost no mixing between the stratosphere and the troposphere beneath it. Ash and gases shot into the stratosphere by a volcanic eruption may remain there for many years.

The stratosphere contains the ozone layer, which lies between 9 and 19 miles (15 and 30 km) from the Earth's surface. Even here, the ozone concentration is quite small, measuring only about 12 ozone molecules for every 1 million air molecules. As small as it is, the ozone concentration is one reason that the stratosphere warms with altitude. The ozone molecules absorb the high-energy UV as they break apart into molecular oxygen (O_2) and atomic oxygen (O).

Air density decreases in the layers of the atmosphere that lie beyond the stratosphere. In each of these layers, the air molecules are very far apart and the air is very cold. Beyond the atmosphere is the **solar wind**, which is made up of high-speed particles traveling rapidly outward from the Sun.

WRAP-UP

The layers of the atmosphere closest to the planet's surface are the troposphere and stratosphere. The troposphere is where life on Earth thrives. Convection currents move air around the troposphere, which is the source of the planet's weather. Above the troposphere is the strato-sphere, which contains the ozone layer, the layer that protects life on Earth from the Sun's dangerous UV radiation. The Earth's atmosphere is much as it has been since plants became abundant hundreds of millions of years ago. Planets without an atmosphere have black skies and no sound.

The Motions
of the Atmosphere

The lower atmosphere is constantly in motion. This movement is responsible for the planet's weather and for transferring heat around the globe. Most atmospheric motions are due to the uneven heating of the Earth by the Sun, since much more solar energy reaches the planet near the equator than at the poles. Convection distributes some of that excess solar heat around the globe. In each hemisphere, the atmosphere has three large convection cells (also known as circulation cells), adding up to six altogether. The major wind belts are located where air at the base of the convection cells moves horizontally along the ground. Where two convection cells meet, air rises or sinks, with the result that there is little wind. The passage of wind in opposite directions at the junction of two convection cells is where some of the world's stormiest weather can be found.

THE BEHAVIOR OF LIGHT

Sunlight is light, not heat. On a warm, sunny day, it is not sunlight that makes the air feel warm, at least not directly. The sunlight is absorbed by the ground surface. This light's energy causes the molecules in the ground to vibrate faster, which increases their temperature and warms the ground. Some of that energy is then emitted as heat. Other substances, including human skin, absorb light energy and convert it to heat. When skin absorbs radiation, it experiences chemical and physical reactions similar to those that take place in cooking; this may result in the skin tanning or burning. Some of the radiation will be reemitted as heat, as can be felt from sunburned skin.

All objects emit electromagnetic radiation. Those that emit at least some of their radiation as visible light, like light bulbs and stars, illuminate. Other objects, like this book, emit radiation in the infrared at wavelengths people cannot see. The book's page is visible because of another property of light—**reflection**. This property is observed when light from a light bulb or the Sun bounces back from a surface, like the page of this book. Some surfaces reflect light better than others; for example, a snowfield reflects a much higher percentage of the light that hits it than a mud pit. The measure of the reflectivity of a surface is called its **albedo**.

Objects appear to have color because they absorb different wavelengths of visible light. For example, an object appears red because it reflects red light; the other colors of light are absorbed. Objects that appear black absorb all visible wavelengths, and those that appear white absorb none. Clearly black objects have lower albedo than white objects.

Besides being absorbed, emitted, and reflected, light also scatters. Incoming sunlight appears white, yet it is made of all the colors of the rainbow. **Scattering** occurs when white light strikes particles—atmospheric gases, water droplets, or dust—then flies out in all directions. The particles may absorb some wavelengths of light. Longer wavelengths are more likely to be absorbed than shorter ones, and so shorter wavelengths are more likely to scatter. Blue wavelengths are shorter than red wavelengths, so blue light scatters more than red light. This is the reason the sky is blue. If the particles do not absorb any wavelengths, the scattered light appears white.

Clouds appear white because tiny water droplets scatter all wavelengths of light. As clouds grow larger and taller, much of the incoming sunlight is reflected and less light penetrates through. This is why the base of a large cloud appears dark. The cloud appears even darker if the droplets at its base grow large enough to absorb rather than scatter light. This often happens before the drops fall to the Earth as rain.

The beautiful reds and oranges of a sunset have a different cause. When the Sun is on the horizon at sunrise and sunset, its rays must travel through a greater thickness of atmosphere than when it is shining overhead. In fact, sunlight must travel through 12 times as much atmosphere when the Sun is at 4° above the horizon than when it is overhead. With this much atmospheric gas to go through, the blue and violet light scatter so much that they are lost. Only the red and orange light make it through, resulting in brilliant red and orange sunsets. The color is more vibrant when the air is full of fine particles, such as dust, volcanic ash, or pollutants. The 1991 eruption of Mt. Pinatubo in the Philippines produced spectacular sunrises and sunsets worldwide.

Rainbows are caused by **refraction**, which is the bending of light as it travels between two different materials. These arcs of color appear to an observer who is between the Sun and some water droplets. Usually this occurs when rain is falling in one part of the sky and the Sun is shining in another, but it also can be seen in a waterfall or the spray from a lawn sprinkler. Since light travels more slowly through water than through air, the light is bent, or refracted, as it moves between the two. The different colors that make up sunlight are refracted at slightly different angles; red light travels fastest so it is refracted the least, while violet light travels the slowest so it is refracted the most. When the light reaches the back of the water drop, it is reflected back; it is refracted again when it passes from the water drop into the air. By the time the journey is over, red light has been bent 42° and violet has been bent 40°, with the rest of the colors—orange, yellow, green, and blue—in between. Each drop appears as only one color; a rainbow is made up of many drops each refracting and reflecting light at slightly different angles. A secondary rainbow, whose color bands are narrower, dimmer, and in the reverse order, may form near the primary

Rainbows are caused by the refraction of sunlight by water droplets to create a spectrum of colors. *(Mr. David Sinson, NOAA, Office of Coast Survey)*

rainbow. This secondary rainbow is created when light is reflected off the back of the drop twice before it exits. Colors in a rainbow are sometimes seen in the sky even when it is not raining; for example, when light refracts through ice crystals.

Few have seen one of the most unusual of atmospheric phenomena, a **mirage**, though many are familiar with cartoons that feature the image of a parched traveler who sights distant palms reflected in a shimmering pond. After crawling across the scorching sand, the traveler is disappointed to discover that, although the palms are there, the pond is just an illusion.

A mirage occurs when the Sun heats the air near the ground so that it is less dense than the air above it. Just as light refracts when it travels between different materials, it also refracts when it travels between layers of air that have different densities. The greater the density difference, the greater the angle of the refraction. As light travels from the top of the palm toward the traveler it hits the hot air layer nearer the ground and is bent upward. The top of the palm appears below its trunk because the light rays coming from the trunk are bent less. So the thirsty traveler perceives the palm as inverted and therefore as reflecting off a pond. This image is intensified by a shimmer that looks like water on the pond's surface, but that is merely caused by light from the sky being bent upward by changes in air density. This shimmer can also be seen while driving on hot highways.

One of the most the spectacular features of the atmosphere is the nighttime **aurora**. Usually found near the poles, the aurora can be brilliant, with streamers, arcs, or fog-like bursts of light, sometimes in white and sometimes in colors, that punctuate the night. These lights are called the aurora borealis, or northern lights, in the Northern Hemisphere and the aurora australis, or southern lights, in the Southern Hemisphere. The aurora occurs because the Earth's magnetic field channels the electrically charged particles of the incoming solar wind to the North and South Poles. As these particles travel through the ionosphere, the part of the Earth's upper atmosphere where free electrons move as electric currents, they collide with the atmospheric gases, causing them to emit light. Each gas emits its own wavelength of light; for example, oxygen emits green or red and nitrogen emits red or violet. The frequency and intensity of the aurora increases during times of intense sunspot activity and solar storms because the solar wind is denser, travels faster, and carries more energy.

THE EARTH'S ENERGY BALANCE

The amount of energy entering the Earth system from the Sun is nearly equal to the amount of energy radiating away from the planet. Solar energy arrives at the top of the Earth's atmosphere as UV or visible light. About 50% of this energy is absorbed, scattered, or reflected by clouds; 3% is reflected by the Earth's surface; and 47%

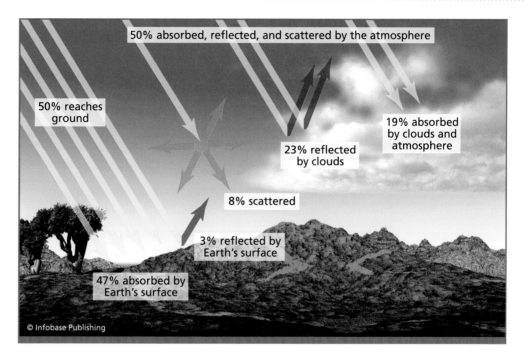

The fate of incoming solar radiation in the atmosphere and at the Earth's surface.

is absorbed by water and land. After being absorbed, the light energy is converted to long-wave, infrared energy, and some of it is reemitted into the atmosphere as heat. If the process stopped there, the planet would just get hotter. This does not happen because eventually the heat is radiated back into space. If the amount of shortwave energy entering the Earth system equals the amount of long-wave radiation leaving the system, the planet's heat budget is in balance. There are two ways this system can be out of balance: When input is greater than output, the planet gets warmer; when output is greater than input, the planet gets cooler.

Although the heat budget of the Earth is, as a whole, fairly well balanced, that is not true for the heat budget at different locations on the surface. For example, solar radiation input varies greatly by **latitude**, which is the distance north or south of the equator as measured in degrees. The equator is at 0° and the poles are at 90° north (90°N) or south (90°S). Overall, the equatorial region takes in more solar radiation than the polar regions. There are three reasons for this:

⊕ First, the polar regions are dark for months at a time in the winter; at the equator, day length shows little seasonal variation.

⊕ Second, near the poles, even in the summer, the Sun never rises very high in the sky, so its rays are filtered through a great wedge of atmosphere before they reach the ground. Near the equator, the midday Sun is always overhead.

⊕ Third, the polar regions are often covered with ice and snow, and so their high albedo measurement means they reflect a high percentage of the solar energy back into the atmosphere.

The amount of solar energy that strikes a region is what determines its average air temperature. The tropics receive much more solar energy than the polar latitudes and therefore they are warmer. It is the imbalance of heat between the low and high latitudes that is the force driving atmospheric circulation.

ATMOSPHERIC CIRCULATION

The atmosphere circulates in great convection cells that begin their motions near the equator. The tropical low pressure zone sucks air horizontally along the ground surface into the gap it leaves. The horizontal motion of air along the ground creates wind. Air in the low pressure zone rises upward to the top of the troposphere then flows toward the poles. As it travels at the top of the atmosphere, the air cools, eventually becoming dense enough to sink, creating a high pressure zone. When it reaches the Earth's surface, the air is sucked toward the equator by the low pressure cell, and warms as it goes. Once at the equator, the convection cell is complete and the air begins its journey again.

In the description above, the low pressure zone was placed at the equator, but the location of the high pressure zone was not given. That is

The Coriolis Effect

The Coriolis effect appears to influence freely moving objects such as baseballs, water, and air molecules. It is not a force itself, but an effect of the Earth's rotation.

The following example makes the Coriolis effect easier to understand. Imagine a baseball game being played on an unmoving turntable. The pitcher standing at the turntable's center throws a ball to a teammate who is standing on the turntable's edge in the 12 o'clock position. The ball flies straight and enters the teammate's mitt. Now, imagine that the turntable is rotating counterclockwise so that the teammate who was at 12 o'clock has reached the 11 o'clock position when the pitcher throws the ball. When the ball reaches the 12 o'clock position, the teammate is not there to catch it. The pitcher is frustrated because, although he threw the ball straight, its path *appears* to have curved to the right relative to the turntable on which he is standing. An observer looking down from above reassures him that the ball did indeed fly straight. No force acted on the ball;

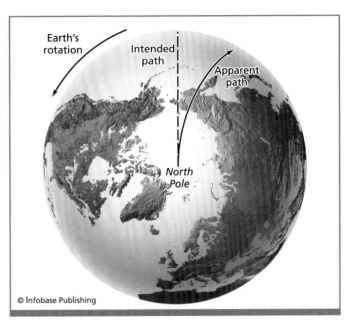

The Coriolis effect appears to deflect winds to the right in the Northern Hemisphere and to the left in the Southern Hemisphere.

the ball appears to have curved because the ground beneath the teammate's feet moved him out of the way.

This example describes the Coriolis effect as viewed from the North Pole. Because the Earth makes one rotation on its axis each day, a point on the equator must travel a much greater distance to get back to its starting point than a point near the pole; as a result, the point at the equator travels at much greater speed. A body traveling from the North Pole toward the

(continues)

(continues)
equator has the slower rotational speed of higher latitudes, and it tends to veer to the west relative to the rapidly rotating planet below. A body traveling toward the North Pole veers eastward because it has the faster rotational speed of the lower latitudes. So, in the Northern Hemisphere, the surface rotates counterclockwise, and moving objects appear to be deflected to the right. In the Southern Hemisphere, objects appear to be deflected to the left and clockwise.

The magnitude of Coriolis deflection depends on the speed of the moving object and its latitude. Faster-moving objects appear to deflect more, as do objects moving near the equator.

because the high pressure zone's location depends on the Earth's rotation. If the planet did not rotate, there would be two high pressure zones, one at the North Pole and one at the South Pole. Atmospheric circulation would consist of one convection cell in the Northern Hemisphere between the equator and the North Pole and another in the Southern Hemisphere between the equator and the South Pole. In reality, the Earth does rotate, which results in the **Coriolis effect**, the tendency of an object to appear to move sideways due to the Earth's rotation.

GLOBAL WIND BELTS

The Coriolis effect modifies global air circulation so that there are six atmospheric circulation cells, three in each hemisphere. At the equator, air behaves as described in the section on atmospheric circulation above. Warm air rises, creating a low pressure cell, and then moves toward the poles at the top of the troposphere. As the air advects poleward, it is deflected by the Coriolis effect—to the right in the Northern Hemisphere and to the left in the Southern Hemisphere. By about 30°N or 30°S, the air has deflected and cooled quite a bit and meets the relatively cool air flowing from the higher latitudes toward the equator. This combined batch of air is relatively cool and dense, so it sinks, creating a high pressure zone. At the ground surface, some of the air circulates back toward the equator to complete the first convection cell. The pattern of air rising at the equator, sinking at the poles, and advecting in between describes the two cells, known as Hadley cells, that circulate air from near the equator to 30°N and 30°S.

Atmospheric circulation cells set the framework for the climate of a region. In locations where the air is rising or sinking, there is little wind. Low pressure zones are the site of a lot of precipitation, and high pressure zones experience more evaporation than precipitation. In the first set of atmospheric circulation cells (the Hadley cells), rising air at the equator causes a great deal of rain and little wind. Early mariners called this region the doldrums because their sailing ships could be becalmed for weeks. The sinking air at 30°N and 30°S is relatively warm since much of it came from the equator and the high pressure cell it creates causes evaporation. On land, these latitudes are where many of the world's great deserts are located, including the Sahara in Africa and the Sonoran Desert in North America. At sea, these regions were named the horse latitudes by Spanish mariners because the lack of wind would sometimes delay their ships for so long that they would run out of water and feed for their livestock, which included horses; the dead horses would be disposed of over the side of the ship.

As the air in the circulation cell moves back toward the equator along the ground, it is deflected by the Coriolis effect. This forms the trade winds, which are referred to as the northeasterly trades in the Northern Hemisphere and the southeasterly trades in the Southern. The trade winds were given their names because they provided a reliable thrust for sailing ships engaging in trade and commerce.

The next two atmospheric circulation cells are located in the middle latitudes. Some of the air that sank at 30°N and 30°S latitude moves along the ground toward the pole. This air is deflected by Coriolis, creating the **westerly winds** or **westerlies** (named for the direction they are coming from). At about 50° to 60°N and 50° to 60°S, this air meets up with air coming from the poles and the whole mass rises, often leading to precipitation. Where these two different air masses come together—one mass indirectly from the equator and the other directly from the pole—is the **polar front**. An

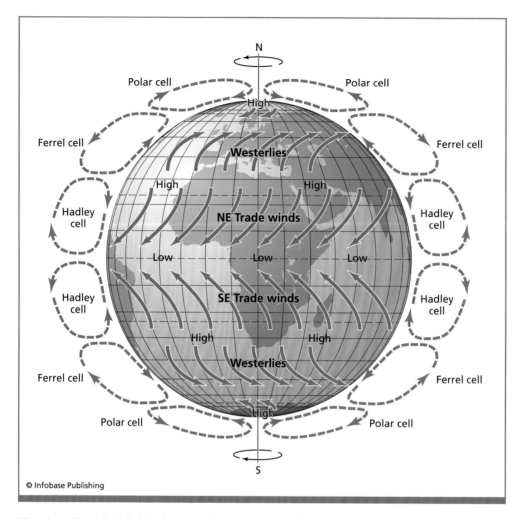

The six-cell model of global air circulation, showing the locations of high and low pressure cells and the directions of the major wind belts on the Earth's surface.

air mass is a large body of air—hundreds of thousands of square miles in area and several miles thick—with similar temperature and humidity throughout (although these features change somewhat with altitude). Because of the arrangement of the different air masses, weather at the polar front is extremely variable, as it is over much of North America and Europe. After the air at the low pressure cell has risen, some of it moves toward the equator. At about 30°N and 30°S, this air meets the air coming from the equator and sinks, completing the second set of circulation cells, known as the Ferrel cells.

Back at the polar front, the air that didn't travel toward the equator moves towards the pole. By the time it reaches the polar region, it is extremely cold and dense, so it sinks. At the surface, it advects toward 60° latitude, completing the third set of circulation cells, known as the polar cells. Winds in the polar cells are deflected by the Coriolis effect, creating the polar easterlies.

In reality, bands of high and low pressure do not encircle the globe but center primarily over the oceans. Over landmasses, which are more abundant in the Northern Hemisphere, many factors can weaken the effects of circulation cells.

JET STREAMS

Jet streams—streams of air suspended in the atmosphere—have an enormous influence on the weather. These rivers of air can travel faster than 100 knots (115 mph, 185 km/hr) and are thousands of miles (km) long, a few hundred miles (km) wide, and only a few miles (km) thick. Jet streams are found at the transition between the troposphere and the stratosphere at heights ranging from 6 to 9 miles (10 to 15 km) above the Earth's surface. Jet streams form when there are great temperature differences between two adjacent air masses. Each hemisphere has two major jet streams: the subtropical jet stream, between the equatorial and midlatitude circulation cells, and the polar jet stream, between the midlatitude and polar circulation cells. Jet streams move with the season. In the Northern Hemisphere, the subtropical jet stream moves from around 20°N in the winter to around 50°N in the summer. The polar jet stream meanders north and south over North America and Europe, dipping as far south as 30°N in the winter and staying up at 50°N to 75°N in the summer.

The polar jet stream has a huge influence on the weather over a large part of North America. If a city is south of the jet stream, it will be under subtropical air; if it is north of the jet stream, it will be under polar air. At the transition between these two zones, the weather is stormy, with the possibility of thunderstorms and tornadoes. The jet stream directs the movement of storms; much weather forecasting involves predicting the jet streams' location and flow. Pilots of eastbound aircraft like the jet stream because it speeds them along, allowing them to save fuel. Pilots of westbound aircraft try to avoid the jet stream, because of the heavy wind resistance.

WRAP-UP

The Earth's atmosphere provides humans with a palette of colors to appreciate: a blue sky, brilliant orange sunsets, dark clouds, rainbows, and the aurora, among other phenomena. Without its atmosphere, the Earth would be a much duller place. Light and its behavior help to determine a region's climate. The amount of sunlight a location receives is the result of its latitude, which also determines where the region is relative to the atmospheric circulation cells and the major wind belts. On the rising or sinking limbs of convection cells there is little wind. Where air rises, precipitation is common, as it is in the equatorial region. Where air sinks, evaporation exceeds precipitation, as in the deserts that encircle the globe at 30°N and 30°S. Jet streams form where circulation cells meet and often are where variable weather and great storms are found.

Other Factors That Shape a Region's Climate

Many other factors besides latitude shape a region's climate. The proximity of a large body of water, such as an ocean, is a major influence, since oceans tend to moderate climate. A land area near an ocean will have a smaller temperature range (the difference between high and low temperature) than one that is farther inland. Climate is also altered by a location's proximity to ocean currents, which distribute heat around the globe. Warm currents traveling to higher latitudes from the equator will warm that region, and cold currents traveling to lower latitudes will similarly cool low-latitude regions. Mountain ranges also affect climate: The weather on the windward side is likely to be wetter than the weather on the leeward side due to water vapor in the air cooling and condensing as it rises upward. After clearing the crest of the range, the air sinks downward, causing it to warm and bring about evaporation.

NOT JUST LATITUDE

If latitude were the only factor controlling climate, all locations at the same latitude would have the same climate. A look at the following table of latitude and climate shows that this is not the case. Although a traveler on a summertime road trip across America at 33°N would be warm all along the way, he or she would go from the warm and breezy California coast at Long Beach, through the sweltering Arizona desert in Phoenix, to the dripping mugginess of Atlanta, Georgia. A traveler on a January trip along the 47th parallel from Seattle to Spokane, Washington, a distance of only 230 miles (370 km) to the east, would be far chillier, likely going from a relatively balmy and wet winter day

Same Latitude, Different Climate

CITY	LATITUDE (°N)	JULY AVERAGE HIGH TEMPERATURE (°F/°C)	JANUARY AVERAGE LOW TEMPERATURE (°F/°C)	AVERAGE ANNUAL PRECIPITATION (INCHES/CM)
Seattle, WA	47	74/23	36/2	36/91
Spokane, WA	47	83/28	20/-7	17/43
Quebec, Canada	47	77/25	3/-16	34/86
San Francisco, CA	37	66/19	46/8	20/51
Wichita, KS	37	92/33	20/-7	29/74
Virginia Beach, VA	37	89/32	31/-1	49/125
Long Beach, CA	33	83/28	48/9	15/38
Phoenix, AZ	33	105/41	40/4	7/18
Atlanta, GA	33	88/31	33/1	50/127

Sources: National Weather Service, National Oceanic and Atmosphere Administration

in Seattle to a much colder and drier one in Spokane. If the traveler continued on to Quebec, Canada, the weather would likely become wetter again, but also a lot colder, and would possibly include snow. The table on page 36 shows the relationship of latitude and climate at three different northern latitudes.

A look at climate differences along latitude lines makes it obvious that other factors play important roles in determining a region's climate. Besides latitude, the temperature and precipitation of a location depend on its position on a continent; where it is relative to mountain ranges; whether it is near an ocean and, if so, what types of ocean currents are nearby.

CONTINENTAL POSITION

The position of a location relative to an ocean is important in determining climate. A location with a maritime climate is influenced by the sea; a location farther inland has a continental climate and is removed from the effects of the ocean. The reasons why the oceans play such a large role in climate include differences in the specific heat of water and rock as well as the moderating effect of the ocean.

Earthy materials—rock, sand, and soil—have a much lower specific heat than water. Land absorbs and releases heat more readily than water and so air temperatures over land are more variable—summer temperatures are hotter and winter temperatures are colder—than air temperatures over water. In a continental climate, there is a great deal of temperature variation from day to night and from summer to winter. In a maritime climate, the ocean moderates temperature so that there is less variation, either daily or seasonally. Temperatures are especially moderate if the prevailing winds come off the sea. For example, San Francisco, California, enjoys cool summers and warm winters because the prevailing winds, called the westerlies, move in from the Pacific Ocean. Although Virginia Beach, Virginia, is at the same latitude on the Atlantic Coast, its climate is much less influenced by the ocean because, in this region, the westerlies come from over the continent. Virginia

Types of Heat

Heat is absorbed or released when a substance changes from one state of matter (solid, liquid, or gas) to another state of matter. The energy released or absorbed when a substance changes its state is called **latent heat**. This means that when a substance changes from one state to another, it releases or absorbs energy.

Water naturally occurs on Earth in all three states of matter. For liquid water to change to solid ice, heat must be removed from the water. For ice to become water, heat must be added to the ice. Adding enough heat to water will turn it into a gas, or water vapor. Taking away enough heat from water vapor transforms it into water. This heat is called latent heat because the temperature of the substance does not change; all of the energy that goes in or out reorganizes the structure of the material.

For example, water on a stove boils—changes from liquid to gas—when its temperature reaches 212°F (100°C). At this temperature, turning up the stove's heat does not increase the water's temperature; liquid water cannot reach a higher temperature. The extra energy—the heat—changes the water from liquid to gas faster. The latent heat required to change water from a liquid to a gas is 540 calories per gram. In other words, once water reaches 212°F (100°C), an additional 540 calories per gram must be added to change the liquid water into steam. The same amount must be taken from steam to change it into liquid water. As another example, the latent heat required to change water from liquid to solid (ice) and back is 80 calories per gram.

Beach summers are hotter and winters are colder than those in San Francisco. Wichita, Kansas, at the same latitude, but in the middle of the United States, has the most extreme climate because it is not influenced by either ocean.

OCEAN CURRENTS

Not only do oceans affect climate, but regions with a maritime or partial maritime climate are influenced by the temperature of the nearby ocean. For example, cool, foggy San Francisco weather is affected by

The concept of latent heat answers important questions about climate. For example, why is March cooler than September in the Northern Hemisphere, even though at any given location the two months have the same day length and the same solar radiation? March is cooler because much of the Sun's incoming energy goes into changing ice to water; that is, into melting snow and ice. (Much of the power of hurricanes comes from latent heat as water vapor transforms into rain.)

Besides latent heat, there is another important heat type. Imagine walking barefoot on a sunny, sandy beach. The sand is hot, but the water is pleasantly cool, although each material is receiving the same amount of solar radiation. There are three reasons for this:

⊕ (1) Water has a much higher specific heat than sand. **Specific heat** is the amount of energy needed to raise the temperature of one gram of material by 1.8°F (1°C). If water and sand absorb equal amounts of solar radiation, the sand becomes hotter than the water.

⊕ Heat disperses more effectively through water because the Sun's rays can penetrate deeper into it. Also, liquid is able to disperse heat by convection while sand is not.

⊕ Water loses heat by **evaporative cooling**, the cooling that takes place as water changes state from a liquid to a gas, due to the latent heat of vaporization.

the cold California Current that flows from the northern Pacific Ocean. But the warm Gulf Stream that runs from the equator up the Atlantic coast of the southeastern United States brings warm, humid weather to Virginia Beach in the summer. So the temperature of nearby ocean currents, which is controlled by where the water is coming from, influence the climate of adjacent lands.

A map of the east–west portions of the surface ocean currents looks a lot like the map of atmospheric circulation. This is because surface currents are driven primarily by the wind, although, of course, the water, being heavier, does not move nearly as fast. For example, the westerlies drag North Pacific water from west to east, while the trade winds north and south of the equator drag surface currents from east to west.

If the Earth were covered entirely by water, surface currents would move in giant belts around the globe. But over most of the planet, the currents run into continents, where they are influenced by the Coriolis effect. As with atmospheric currents, surface currents turn to the right in the Northern Hemisphere and to the left in the Southern Hemisphere. The currents continue to travel along the continent until they run into an east–west flowing current going in the opposite direction. The result is that surface currents travel in loops called **gyres**, which rotate clockwise in the Northern Hemisphere and counterclockwise in the Southern Hemisphere.

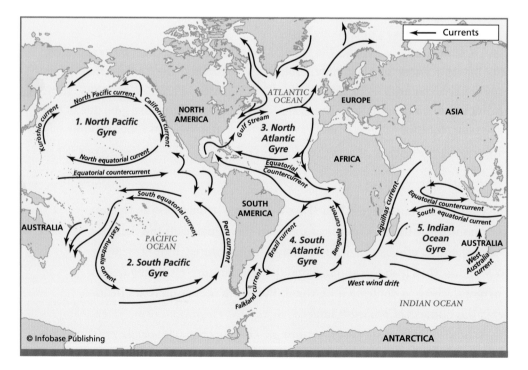

The major surface ocean currents. The five gyres are the North and South Pacific, the North and South Atlantic, and the Indian.

As discussed in the San Francisco and Virginia Beach examples, ocean currents alter the temperature of the air above them. The North Equatorial Current, which is warmed by the Sun as it travels from east to west in the Atlantic Ocean from the equator, turns north when it hits the Americas to become the Gulf Stream. This large, swift warm-water current raises air temperatures as it moves northward along the eastern United States and southeastern Canada. The current then swings away from North America and heads east toward Europe as the North Atlantic Drift. Once it arrives, it divides into two currents. One moves south along Europe and flows back toward the equator. The other travels north along Britain and Norway, bringing relatively warm water to the northern latitudes. This process has an enormous effect on the climate of northern Europe. Although London is at 51°N latitude, several degrees north of Quebec, the climate there is much more temperate, with rain instead of snow as the dominant winter precipitation.

NEARBY MOUNTAINS

Air temperature decreases with increasing altitude because there are fewer molecules to collide with each other and less heat is generated. So the air atop a mountain range is typically colder than the air at its base. But altitude is not the only way mountain ranges shape climate. Mountain ranges have two additional effects, both of which are especially apparent if the mountains are near a coastal area. The first is obvious: If the mountain range separates the coastal region from the continent, the moderating influence of the ocean is limited to the windward side of the range.

The second effect is the **rain shadow** effect. As maritime air rises over the windward side of the mountains, the air cools. Cooler air holds less moisture, so rain or snow may fall, which dries the air. As the air descends down the leeward side of the mountains, it warms. In this high pressure cell, evaporation may exceed precipitation, so the weather on the leeward side of the range is relatively warm and dry. The Sierra Nevada range of California is a good example of the effects of mountain ranges on local climate. The west side of the Sierras is wet and forested,

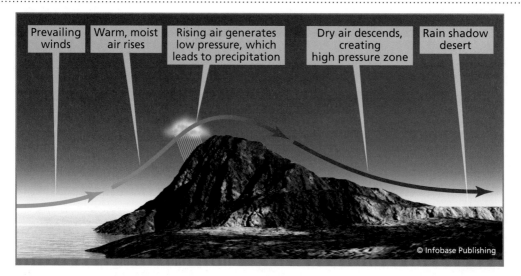

Rain shadow effect. Warm moist air from over the ocean rises and cools over a mountain range, resulting in precipitation. The air descends dry and hot to create a desert on the leeward side of the range.

including forests of towering Sequoia trees, but on the east side is the Great Basin, a desert known for its sagebrush and tumbleweeds.

WRAP-UP

Factors besides latitude have a large effect on the climate of a region. The presence or absence of a nearby ocean will determine if the climate is moderate, as with a maritime climate, or if it is more extreme, as with a continental climate. The temperature of the nearby ocean currents also influence nearby climate. One dramatic example is found in the British Isles, which are much balmier than other locations at similar latitudes, because of the Gulf Stream that flows into the North Atlantic from the equator. Mountain ranges also influence climate, in part, because they restrict the moderating effects of sea air to their windward side. In addition, the windward side of a range is likely to be cooler and wetter than the leeward side because of how the moisture in the air condenses and falls as precipitation as it rises up the slope, until it crosses over to the leeward side, where it becomes warmer and drier.

PART TWO

ATMOSPHERIC BEHAVIOR: THE WEATHER

What Makes
the Weather?

A detailed weather report includes information about the temperature and humidity of the air, the wind speed and direction, the percentage of cloud cover, and the amount and type of precipitation. Many factors influence the weather of a particular region. Among them are what type of air mass the region is beneath, whether the region is located where two air masses meet, and the proximity of high and low pressure cells.

Weather is different from climate. Weather is the condition of the atmosphere at a particular time and place, while climate is the long-term average of weather conditions. Tucson, Arizona, for example, has a warm, desert climate, but a winter day might include a rare snowstorm.

AIR MASSES

The temperature and humidity of a region on a given day depend largely on the characteristics of the air mass that lies above it. An air mass forms when air sits over a region for several days or longer

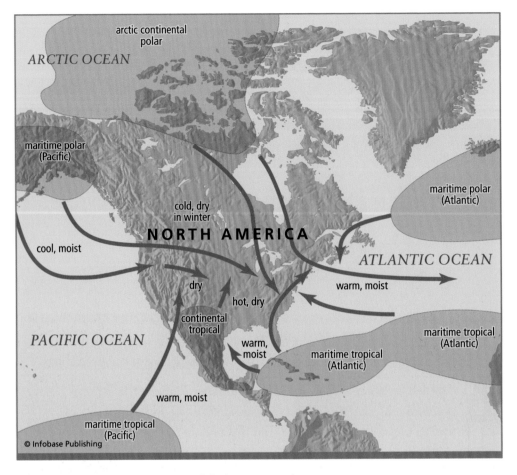

Air masses over North America and their source regions.

and acquires the distinctive temperature and humidity of that region. This happens because heat and moisture are transferred between the ground surface and the air above it until the air has the same characteristics as the ground. For example, air masses that form over oceans are moister than those that form over continents; those that form over polar regions are colder than those that form over the tropics.

When an air mass leaves the place where it formed, it brings its distinctive temperature and humidity characteristics to its new location. Stormy weather may result if the characteristics of the air mass are different from those of the new region. When a cold air mass moves over warm ground, for example, the bottom of the air mass is heated. The warmed air then rises, leading to clouds, rain, and possibly thunderstorms. When a warm air mass travels over cold ground, the bottom of the mass cools and forms a temperature inversion, in which air temperature increases with altitude. Inversions trap air, including pollutants, over a region because the cold air near the ground cannot rise into the warm air above it.

FRONTS

A region may be stormy at the meeting place of two air masses, known as a **front**, especially if the two air masses are very different. There

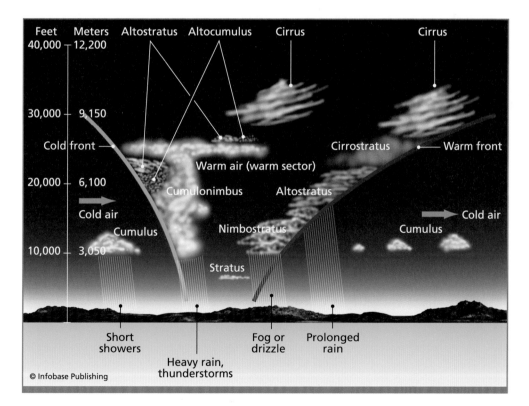

In a warm front, a warm air mass rises over a cold front, producing cumulus and cumulo-nimbus clouds and violent precipitation. In a cold front, warm air slides upward over cold air at a warm front. Stratus and cirrus clouds form, the former producing gentle rain.

are several types of fronts. For example, **stationary fronts** are those in which the air masses do not move—rain, drizzle, and fog can sit over the same area for several days. **Occluded fronts** form when a fast-moving cold air mass traps a warm air mass against a second cold air mass and lifts it off the ground, resulting in precipitation where the air masses of different temperatures meet.

As a front travels over a region, one air mass replaces the other. A **warm front** is where the warm air takes over the position of the cold air. The warm air rises, producing clouds and precipitation, occasionally even thunderstorms. Warm fronts advance slowly, at only about 15 miles (25 km) per hour. A **cold front** is where cold air takes over the position of the warm air and pushes it upward. Cold fronts advance faster, at about 22 miles (35 km) per hour, and are associated with violent weather such as intense thunderstorms.

CLOUDS

Clouds have a tremendous influence on weather; they break up sunny days by blocking sunlight or by causing rain, snow, hail, lightning, and rainbows. Clouds are made up of tiny water droplets with an average diameter of 0.00078 inches (0.002 centimeters) or ice crystals suspended in the atmosphere. Clouds filter out incoming solar radiation and absorb warmth that is reradiated up from the ground. Cloudy days

Cloud Names

CLOUD NAME	LATIN MEANING	CLOUD FORM
Stratus	Layer	Sheetlike
Cumulus	Heap	Puffy
Cirrus	Curl of hair	Wispy
Nimbus	Violent rain	Rain cloud

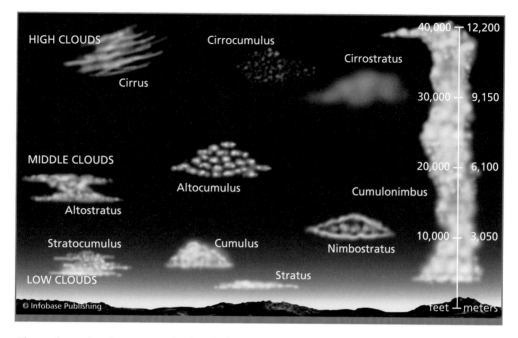

The various cloud types are depicted above.

have a more moderate **temperature range**—the difference between daily high and low temperature—than cloudless days.

Almost all clouds are found in the troposphere. They are classified by their appearance into 4 main groups, as shown in the table on page 48. These 4 main groups contain 10 cloud types, classified by appearance and height above the ground.

High clouds reside at greater than 20,000 feet (6,100 m). They form where air is frigid and there is little water vapor; hence, they are thin and composed entirely of ice crystals. White, feathery cirrus clouds are the most common cloud type at this altitude. They appear as long, windblown streamers called mares' tails. Cirrus clouds may warn of an approaching storm. Cirrocumulus clouds are small, white puffs found in lines rippling across the sky. Sheetlike cirrostratus clouds are white and thin. They bend the incoming rays of the Sun or light from the Moon, creating a halo around them. Thicker cirrostratus clouds indicate rain or snow within the next 24 hours.

Middle clouds, located between 6,500 and 23,000 feet (2,000 and 7,000 m), are composed of water vapor or ice crystals. Altocumulus clouds are gray, puffy blobs seen as bands rolling across the sky; they often herald late afternoon thunderstorms. Altostratus clouds are thick and broad and precede storms that bring widespread, nearly nonstop precipitation.

Low clouds form below 6,500 feet (2,000 m). They are composed of water droplets and contain some ice and snow in very cold weather. Stratus clouds usually cover the entire sky but rarely produce rain. Thick and dark nimbostratus clouds drop light to moderate rain or snow. Usually, stratocumulus clouds form as lines of fairly large, rounded clumps, ranging from white to gray.

The fourth group of clouds develops vertically more than horizontally. Cumulus clouds are white puffs with a flat base and a cauliflower-like head. Cumulus clouds grow as condensing

Ominous clouds at a weather front. *(NOAA Photo Library, NOAA Central Library; OAR/ERL/ National Severe Storms Laboratory)*

water vapor creates vertical air currents. If their vertical currents strengthen, cumulus clouds grow into towering cumulonimbus clouds, the dramatic clouds of thunderstorms that are accompanied by rain, snow, hail, and lightning.

The stratosphere is too dry for cloud formation except during extremely chilly polar winters. At that time, **polar stratospheric clouds (PSCs)** form at very high altitudes, about 70,000 feet (21,000 m). Composed of water and nitric acid, these iridescent clouds are essential for breaking down chlorine-containing compounds, such as CFCs, in the stratosphere. Even higher in the polar stratosphere are **noctilucent clouds,** which are composed of tiny ice crystals and may form from the breakdown of methane gas.

For air at any humidity level, there is a temperature below which water vapor will begin to condense into liquid water. This temperature is called the **dew point**. Since air cools as it rises and cool air holds less moisture than warm air, rising air will reach its dew point at a particular altitude. This altitude is known as its **condensation level**, which depends on the air's temperature and humidity. The flat under-sides of many clouds reveal the location of the condensation level for that air. If rising air continues to chill, the water droplets may freeze into ice.

Clouds form in the three different ways listed below. All involve the rising of warm air.

- ⊕ Warm air rising from the ground exceeds its dew point, creating a cumulus cloud. As the rising air cools, it moves away from the center of the cloud then sinks back down to the ground, creating a convection cell. If the air above the condensation level is stable, the cloud will be small. If the air continues to rise, the cloud will mushroom into a cumulonimbus cloud. If the cloud reaches the stratosphere, it can no longer grow upward and instead grows outward, creating a flat, anvil-shaped summit.

- ⊕ Warm air is pushed upward at a mountain or mountain range. If the humidity is high enough, clouds form and may precipitate. As the air descends on the other side of the mountains, it warms, causing the rain shadow effect.

⊕ Warm air is wedged upward by a mass of cold air. This forms a front, which may be characterized by clouds that cover hundreds or thousands of square miles.

PRECIPITATION

The presence or absence of precipitation—dew, rain, snow, sleet, hail, and frost—is a major feature of weather. Dew forms on surfaces that cool the surrounding air to below its dew point. Frost forms if the air cools below its freezing point. The other types of precipitation come from clouds. In warm clouds, water droplets suspended in updrafts collide with other rising droplets and then grow so large that gravity forces them to fall. Violent storms have strong updrafts, so droplets remain suspended until they are quite large. Drops may become smaller once they begin to fall. Raindrops sometimes break apart or, if they fall through a warm sky, may partially or wholly evaporate.

In the middle-to-upper portions of cold clouds, where the temperature is around 14°F (-10°C), a tiny number of water droplets freeze into ice crystals. The rest of the water remains as extremely cold water vapor, which joins the ice crystals without first becoming liquid. When the ice crystals become heavy enough they fall, collecting more droplets as they descend. If temperatures are cold and the ice crystals stick together, they form a snowflake. Snowflakes become raindrops when warm surface temperatures melt the snow before it reaches the ground.

When raindrops fall through a layer of frigid air near the ground, they freeze to become sleet. If the drops freeze onto a surface, they form glaze. Glaze can be heavy enough to cause a tree branch to fall under its weight. Ice particles that grow as they circle around in convection cells in cumulonimbus clouds create hail. When hail becomes too heavy, it falls to the ground. Although hail is usually less than

0.5 inch (1 cm) in diameter, hail that is 2 to 4 inches (5 to 10 cm) in diameter is not uncommon.

FOG

Fog forms when humid air near the ground cools below its dew point. Fog not only influences weather, it sometimes plays a role in the defining character of a region. For example, San Francisco is famous for its **advection fog**, which forms as warm, wet air over the Pacific Ocean blows eastward over the cold California Current. Just before it reaches the California coastline, the air cools below its dew point, and the fog is brought onshore by breezes coming inland from the sea. On windy days, the fog can mushroom to 2,000 feet (600 m) thick.

San Francisco's famous advection fog forms as warm, wet air from over the Pacific is cooled below its dew point as it passes over the cold California Current. *(Historic NWS Collection)*

There are several other types of fog. **Radiation fog** originates on clear nights when warm, moist air is cooled by the ground. Breezes carry the water particles upward, so radiation fogs can grow up to 100 feet (30 m) thick. **Upslope fog** forms when warm, humid air travels up a hillside. **Steam fog** forms in autumn when cool air moves over a lake that has retained some of its summer heat.

LOCAL WINDS

Wind is another major element of weather and may define the character of one region as much as fog defines another. Wind is created by air moving from zones of high pressure to zones of low pressure. The greater the difference in pressure between the two zones, the greater the wind speed will be.

A variety of conditions brings about the formation of high and low pressure cells and generates wind. Winds can be created by the temperature differences between land and sea. In the winter, air over a continent is cold and dense, creating a high pressure zone. Air over a nearby ocean is relatively warm and light, creating a low pressure zone. In the winter, air blowing from the cooler land to the warmer ocean creates **land breezes**. In the summer, high and low pressure cells are reversed so **sea breezes** blow cooler ocean air over the warmer land; sea breezes can lower the air temperature over land as much as 9° to 18°F (5° to 10°C). Land and sea breezes help to moderate coastal climates as much as 30 to 60 miles (50 to 100 km) inland.

Winds also may form up and down mountain slopes. During the day, air above a mountain slope is heated more than air suspended over the adjacent valley. The warm air rises, drawing a breeze, known as a **valley breeze**, uphill. These updrafts bring late afternoon thunderstorms to mountainous regions. At night, air over the mountain slopes cools more quickly than the air over the nearby valley, so it sinks, bringing a **mountain breeze** downhill.

Chinook winds are caused by low pressure on the leeward side of a mountain range that draws air over the mountains. The air loses its moisture on the windward side and descends into the valley as a warm, dry wind. Chinooks are common in the Rocky Mountains, where air temperature on the eastern slope may rise 36°F (20°C) and cause a rapid melting of snow. The well-known Santa Ana winds of southern California are also Chinook–type winds. They bring hot,

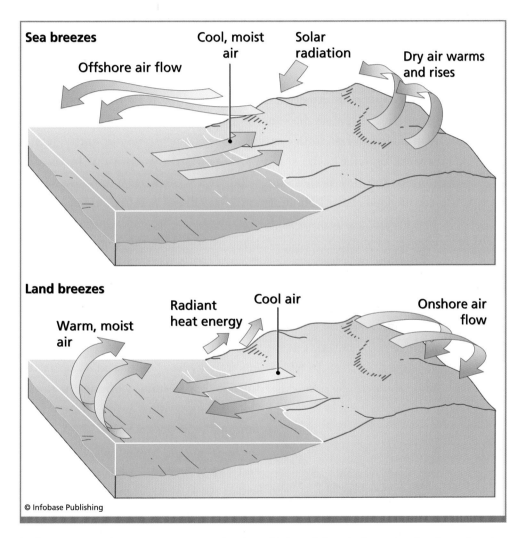

Sea breezes

Offshore air flow

Cool, moist air

Solar radiation

Dry air warms and rises

Land breezes

Warm, moist air

Radiant heat energy

Cool air

Onshore air flow

© Infobase Publishing

In the summer, air temperatures over land are high and the air rises, drawing in cooler air from the adjacent ocean and creating sea breezes. In the winter, warmer temperatures over water cause the air to rise and draw in cooler air from the adjacent land, creating land breezes.

dry air into the region at the end of its drought season, often fueling devastating fires.

EL NIÑO EVENTS

El Niño events also have a temporary effect on weather; these effects may be both regional and global. Some of the most profound short-term changes in global climate take place during an El Niño. These events are caused by the reversing of the atmospheric and oceanic currents in the equatorial Pacific Ocean. In a normal year, the Peru Current travels up South America from the frigid waters that flow around Antarctica. Because the water is very cold, it is also dense, and deep sea water can rise to the surface. Deep water is rich in nutrients and when it upwells to the surface, **phytoplankton** thrive. (Phytoplankton are the tiny photosynthesizing plants that form the base of the marine food chain.) The water then travels north to the equator, where descending air forms a high pressure cell. The current warms as the trade winds drag the water across the Pacific along the equator. By the time the water reaches the western Pacific, it is very warm. Some of this water joins currents moving north and south, while some moves back across the Pacific as a countercurrent. The rest piles up in the western Pacific and continues to warm; the air above this warm water rises, forming a low pressure cell.

In time, the two atmospheric pressure cells weaken, causing the trade winds to weaken or reverse direction. The reversed trade winds drag warm water rapidly from west to east, enhancing the countercurrent. When this warm water hits South America, it spreads over the cooler, denser water at the sur-

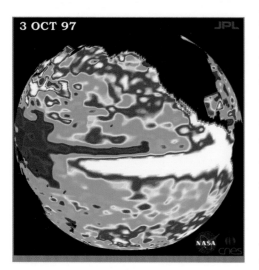

Sea surface temperatures during an El Niño year. The water off of South America is much warmer, and the ribbon of water flowing across the equator is hot. *(TOPEX / Poseidon, NASA JPL)*

face, and nutrient-rich deep water can no longer rise to the surface. (El Niño was named for the Christ child by Spanish fishermen because the phenomenon often begins around Christmas.)

El Niño events have both local and global effects. Without cold, nutrient-rich water off of South America, the phytoplankton population collapses. This collapse disturbs the food chain and causes the deaths of many fish and other organisms. The 1972 El Niño triggered the collapse of Peru's once-bountiful anchovy fishery, which was already suffering from years of overfishing. Sea bird and some marine mammal populations also collapsed.

During El Niño events, some regions, such as Ecuador and northern Peru,

Sea surface temperatures during a La Niña year. Cool water travels up South America and across the equatorial Pacific in a ribbon. *(TOPEX / Poseidon, NASA JPL)*

receive a great increase in their normal rainfall, and the coastal desert is transformed into grassland, which disturbs the normal **ecosystem** (An ecosystem includes the plants and animals of a region and the resources they need to live). In the western, southern, and northeastern United States, great storms bring floods and landslides. Flooding also occurs over large parts of South America and Western Europe. At the same time, drought strikes other parts of South America, plus the western Pacific, southern and northern Africa, southern Asia, and southern Europe.

An El Niño event ends about one to two years after it begins, when most of the warm western Pacific waters have moved east. When the event is over, normal circulation patterns resume in both the atmosphere and the ocean. Sometimes, during the recovery, the air and water move to the west more vigorously than normal and unusually cold water accumulates in the eastern Pacific. This situation is called **La Niña**.

OTHER INFLUENCES ON WEATHER

Volcanic eruptions may have a temporary influence on weather. Very large, explosive eruptions inject massive amounts of gases and dust into the atmosphere. The gases and dust block incoming sunlight and affect weather globally. In this way, the 1815 eruption of Mount Tambora in Indonesia brought on the very cold "year without a summer."

Forests influence both local and global weather. On a hot day, a large tree may extract up to 5 tons (5.5 metric tons) of water and transpire it into the atmosphere where it forms rain clouds. In all, 50% to 80% of the moisture above a tropical rain forest comes from the trees. Forests also act as sponges for water. They slow runoff and absorb water that later enters streams and groundwater. If forests are cleared, the ground becomes dry and open to erosion.

WRAP-UP

Weather describes the state of the atmosphere in a given location at a particular time. Many features influence the weather of a location, including the temperature and humidity of the overlying air mass, its proximity to a front, the percentage and type of cloud cover, and the amount and type of precipitation. Although weather is highly variable, there are limits to what might be expected at a particular location. Alterations to the atmosphere may expand weather possibilities at a location for a matter of months or years. Most striking are El Niño events, which occur as the trade winds along the equatorial Pacific weaken or reverse direction. These atmospheric perturbations bring extreme rains to some locations and intense droughts to others. Particles from massive volcanic eruptions may block the Sun, causing winterlike conditions; the loss or gain of forests can change the precipitation patterns of a region.

Extreme Weather

This chapter looks at thunderstorms, hurricanes, extreme heat, droughts, and other types of extreme weather. For most regions, some extreme weather is part of the array of atmospheric activity that is considered normal. Some weather events are rare enough and severe enough that they are always newsworthy (hurricanes that reach land are a good example). Other events are only of regional interest; the arrival of the summer monsoon makes the news for days in southern Arizona but is of little concern to the rest of the country, unless the monsoon brings intense flooding to a major population center. The most frequent events—thunderstorms, for example—are likely to be of only local interest, unless they are especially destructive. Extreme weather is common enough to be familiar but uncommon enough to capture our attention when it happens.

THUNDERSTORMS AND TORNADOES

Thunderstorms are so common in some locations that they can hardly be considered extreme. Each year, our planet hosts about 14 million of these wild tempests, which averages to 40,000 thunderstorms a day.

Although they can be extremely powerful and do a great deal of damage, thunderstorms are relatively small compared to other powerful storms such as cyclones. Thunderheads form individually or along the length of a cold front that can be as long as 600 miles (1,000 km). The most dangerous storms along such a **squall line** can grow to more than 50,000 feet (15 km) high. In the United States, squall lines form in the spring and early summer where the warm, humid air mass from the Gulf of Mexico meets the frigid continental air mass from Canada.

Thunderstorms are named for the earsplitting clap that accompanies the lightning strikes they create. Lightning is a powerful discharge of electricity. It may strike within a cloud, between clouds, between a

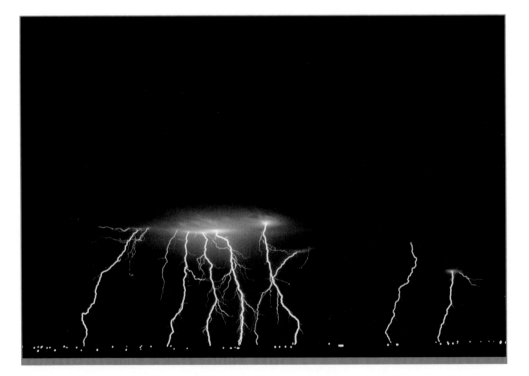

Lightning strikes in many spots during an intense storm. *(NOAA Photo Library, NOAA Central Library; OAR/ERL/National Severe Storms Laboratory)*

cloud and the surrounding air, or from a cloud to the ground. Luckily, only about 20% of lightning bolts strike the ground. Thunderstorms generate winds that damage crops and property, hail that pummels crops, heavy rains that bring flash floods, lightning that strikes people and ignites forest fires, and tornadoes that destroy local areas. Approximately 200 Americans die and 550 are injured by lightning strikes each year. One common misconception is that lightning does not strike the same place twice—in fact, it strikes New York City's Empire State Building about 23 times per year.

Thunderstorms are classified as either ordinary or severe. Ordinary thunderstorms are shorter-lived and milder than severe thunderstorms. These common storms build above warm ground, so they form most often in the late afternoon or early evening, in spring and summer. The storms are born when masses of warm, humid air rise into an unstable atmosphere. If these updrafts are extremely strong, cumulus clouds, followed by cumulonimbus clouds, swell upward. When the cloud top reaches the stratosphere, the winds shift it horizontally, forming the anvil shape of a thunderhead. Condensing water vapor in the rising air releases latent heat until the air inside the cloud is warmer than the air outside. The powerful updrafts keep water droplets and ice crystals suspended until they grow so large that they fall as rain or hail. The rain and hail cool the cloud as they descend, and the cooler air becomes dense and begins to sink, setting up a downdraft. This downdraft and the original updraft make up the two vertical limbs of a convection cell. Most thunderstorms have several convection cells; the side-by-side updrafts and downdrafts create wind shear. By now, the thunderstorm is mature, producing gusty winds, lightning, heavy rain, and hail. Although now extremely impressive, this thunderstorm is doomed. Cool temperatures at the base of the cloud weaken convection, cutting off the updraft of moist air and ending condensation. Without its source of latent heat, the storm dies, usually between 15 and 30 minutes after it began, although new thunderheads often build in the same region.

Severe thunderstorms are similar but more intense. In the United States, severe thunderstorms are most common in the Midwest but may occur in other locations. Severe thunderstorms have extremely strong updrafts, so raindrops and hailstones become huge before becoming heavy enough to fall. Severe thunderstorms have hail that is at least 0.75 inch (1.9 cm) in diameter and surface wind gusts of nearly 60 mph (97 km/hr). Once the hail falls, the intense precipitation of a severe thunderstorm cools the base of the cloud so much that severe downdrafts form. Rather than signaling the demise of the thunderstorm, these robust downdrafts strike the ground and wedge warm air upward, enhancing the updrafts. These convection cells are so powerful that they can keep a storm alive for many hours.

Sometimes the downdrafts hit the ground and spread horizontally, creating a **microburst**. In a microburst, winds may reach 170 mph (170 km/hr), damaging trees, buildings, and other structures. Microbursts were discovered in 1985 when a Delta Airlines jumbo jet attempted to

Cumulonimbus squall line associated with a cold front. *(Historic NWS Collection)*

land at Dallas–Fort Worth Airport, Texas, during a summer thunderstorm. As the plane made its final approach, the storm intensified and the aircraft was slammed down on the ground far short of the runway, smashing a car and killing 137 of the people on board the plane. Reviews of data from previous airplane crashes revealed that other

A tornado strikes south of Dimmitt, Texas, in June 1995. *(NOAA Photo Library, NOAA Central Library; OAR/ERL/National Severe Storms Laboratory)*

planes were probably downed by microbursts. Pilots are now trained to detect and maneuver through these perilous winds.

The extreme wind shear in a severe thunderstorm causes the air mass to rotate, sometimes spawning tornadoes. These violently rotating, funnel-shaped clouds extend below the cumulonimbus cloud of the thunderstorm toward the ground surface. Tornadoes are intense—the winds may exceed 200 to 300 miles (320 to 480 km) per hour in speed—but they are relatively small, only a few feet to a mile in diameter. The updraft at the center may reach 200 miles (320 km) per hour. Tornadoes are found in great numbers along what is known as Tornado Alley, an area running through the states of Nebraska, Kansas, Oklahoma, and Texas.

Tornadoes grow along squall lines, with multiple storms occurring at the same time. In April 1974, a squall line produced 148 tornadoes—the largest number ever recorded for a 24-hour period—over 2,600 miles, through 13 states and Canada. During the peak of the storm, 15 tornadoes were on the ground simultaneously. The death toll was 315 people, with nearly 5,500 injured.

Meteorologist and Storm Chaser: *Alan Moller*

Alan Moller's earliest memories of thunderstorms are from a tragic day in 1954 when he was four years old. While going to visit relatives, his family was in a severe traffic accident, and his mother was killed. The family spent the night with a doctor in a small town in eastern Indiana that was experiencing severe thunderstorms. Large tree limbs were blown down, and there was lightning from a new storm. The destruction he witnessed from the storms and from the accident became entangled in his memory. Four years later, Alan saw a TV program called *Our Friend the Weather*, with incredible film footage of a 1957 tornado in Dallas, Texas—it was then that he became hooked for life.

As a meteorology student at Oklahoma University, Moller was invited to join the Tornado Intercept Project. This first official "storm chase" took place during the 1972 to 1974 spring tornado periods. Run by the National Severe Storm Laboratory in Norman, Oklahoma, and the meteorology department at the university, the project's goal was to intercept tornadic thunderstorms to determine whether Doppler radar would be useful as a warning tool for tornadoes. Conventional radar detects a storm's type and intensity of precipitation; these studies showed that Doppler radar also can detect the presence of circular motions in a storm that may indicate a developing tornado.

Since 1974, Moller has worked for the National Weather Service (NWS) as a severe storm researcher and forecaster. His primary responsibilities have been developing training programs for volunteer storm spotters to recognize tornadoes (from a safe viewpoint), as well as to identify and report large hail, damaging winds, and flash flooding. NWS meteorologists interpret the radar, and the spotters interpret and report severe weather as it occurs. This works well, because Doppler radar cannot "see" a tornado, and spotters cannot "see" a developing tornadic circulation in the clouds. Working together, Doppler radar and volunteer storm spotters, who are mainly amateur radio operators, are the backbones of the tornado warning system in the United States.

Now a senior forecaster at the NWS forecast office in Fort Worth, Texas, Moller has written or cowritten about 30 scientific papers and has won many awards. His main hobbies are storm chasing, landscape and weather photography, and hiking.

THE MONSOON

Monsoon describes a seasonal wind pattern that is a larger scale version of the land and sea breezes discussed in Chapter 5. As with land and sea breezes, monsoon winds change direction with the change of season, blowing onto the land in summer and away from it in winter. Monsoons are found in the coastal regions of all continents where summer temperatures are extremely high.

The most important monsoon in the world occurs in the summer over the extremely hot Indian subcontinent. The more than two billion residents of India and southeastern Asia depend on these monsoon rains for their drinking and irrigation water. When the air above the scorching hot Indian subcontinent rises, it draws in warm, humid air from the northern Indian Ocean, along with air from drier continental regions. As it rises, the humid sea air unleashes extremely heavy rains. In Cherrapunji, India—dubbed the wettest place on Earth in most years—the average annual rainfall is 428 inches (1,087 cm). The air pattern then reverses in the winter and cool air from over the land moves seaward. In earlier times, traders used seasonal shifts in the monsoon winds to propel their sailing ships back and forth between India and Africa.

CYCLONES

Cyclones are much larger but less common than thunderstorms and tornadoes. A **cyclone** is a system of winds rotating around a low pressure center. These winds circulate counterclockwise in the Northern Hemisphere and clockwise in the Southern Hemisphere due to the Coriolis effect. At the center of the cell, air rises and cools, causing clouds and rain. There are two types of cyclones: the typical winter storms of the mid-latitudes and the more intense late-summer storms of the tropical regions, which are also known as hurricanes. The opposite of a cyclone is an **anticyclone**, in which winds spiral outward from a high pressure cell. Anticyclones are weaker than cyclones and are usually associated with sunshine.

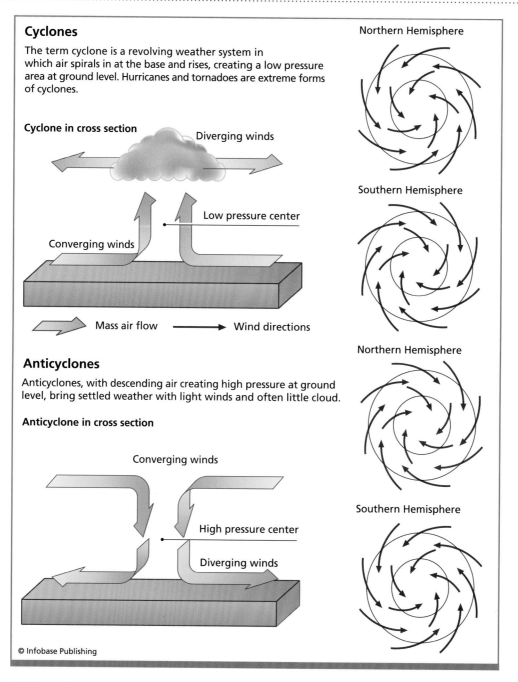

Cyclones

The term cyclone is a revolving weather system in which air spirals in at the base and rises, creating a low pressure area at ground level. Hurricanes and tornadoes are extreme forms of cyclones.

Cyclone in cross section

Diverging winds

Low pressure center

Converging winds

Mass air flow   Wind directions

Anticyclones

Anticyclones, with descending air creating high pressure at ground level, bring settled weather with light winds and often little cloud.

Anticyclone in cross section

Converging winds

High pressure center

Diverging winds

Northern Hemisphere

Southern Hemisphere

Northern Hemisphere

Southern Hemisphere

© Infobase Publishing

(TOP) Air flows into a low pressure cell. As the air in the cell rises, it cools and creates clouds and precipitation, creating a cyclone. *(BOTTOM)* Air flows out of a high pressure cell and forms an anticyclone. The sinking air creates clear skies.

Mid-latitude Cyclones

Mid-latitude cyclones—wind systems that rotate around a low pressure center in the middle latitudes—are large and abundant. These storms are the main cause of day-to-day weather changes in the middle to high latitudes. Most mid-latitude cyclones develop along the polar front, where polar and tropical air masses blow past each other in opposite directions. As winds come into the polar front from both sides, they are deflected by the Coriolis effect (to the right in the Northern Hemisphere; to the left in the Southern Hemisphere), so they strike the polar front at an angle. Consequently, a warm front forms on one side and a cold front on the other. At the cold front, the warm air rises and creates a low pressure cell. As the low pressure cell intensifies, winds rush to its center and rise in a twisting mass that releases a great deal of precipitation.

Mid-latitude cyclones are the main cause of winter storms in the temperate regions. Lasting two to five days, they can reach 625 to 1,600 miles (1,000 to 2,500 km) in diameter and produce winds of up to 75 miles (125 km) per hour. These storms move with the westerly winds and bring dramatic weather changes over an area of several hundred to a few thousand miles (km). In the mid-Atlantic and New England states, they are called **Nor'easters** (northeasters) because they blow in from the northeast. Each year, about 30 Nor'easters bring Atlantic Ocean moisture to the eastern seaboard and dump it as snow, rain, or ice. Sometimes these storms are fierce: Heavy snow and ice may precede warm rains that freeze onto the cold ground surface, creating a cloak of ice that can paralyze this densely populated area, bring about extensive flooding, and sometimes even cause deaths.

The three-day-long Nor'easter that struck the United States from West Virginia to Connecticut in December 1992 was called a 100-year storm—a storm so rare in its severity that one of its magnitude likely occurs only once every 100 years. Cape May, New Jersey, experienced the storm's highest winds of 80 miles (130 km) per hour. The tidal surge at that location was 1 to 4 feet (0.4 to 1.2 m), and the waves reached heights of 20 to 25 feet (6.1 to 7.6 m). Snowfall of 27 inches (70 cm) in 24 hours coated the hills west of Boston, and 4 feet (1.2 m) of snow buried the Berkshire Mountains of western Massachusetts. Floodwaters of 4 to 5 feet (1.2 to 1.5 m) submerged portions of Boston and New York City. Four deaths were attributed to the storm.

Hurricanes

Tropical cyclones have many different names because they arise in nearly all tropical oceans. Called hurricanes in the North Atlantic and eastern Pacific oceans, they go by the name *typhoon* in the western Pacific, *tropical cyclone* in the Indian Ocean, and *willi-willi* in the oceans around Australia. Tropical cyclones are the costliest and most dangerous storms on the Earth.

Hurricanes in the Northern Hemisphere originate within the easterly trade winds (10 to 25°N) in summer and autumn. For a hurricane to be born and to grow, a vast area of the sea surface must be 82°F (28°C) or higher, and there must be only light winds. A large, humid air mass grows over the warm sea and creates a low pressure cell that thunderstorms organize around. If temperatures within the cell rise high enough, the air begins to rotate counterclockwise. The storm mushrooms upward as hot, spiraling columns of warm air feed on heat energy from the tropical waters. For the storm to become massive, wind shear between the lower and upper atmosphere must be low. If wind shear is high, the storm will be decapitated. When conditions are right, the latent heat released by cloud formation will give the storm the energy to become a killer.

Hurricanes are huge, roughly 350 miles (600 km) in diameter and 50,000 feet (15 km) high. A hurricane has winds of at least 74 miles (118 km) per hour, except within the 8- to 10-mile (20- to 50- km) wide eye of the storm—an area that is remarkably calm because the air is rising vertically. Besides the high winds and rain, hurricanes spawn tornadoes. Rainfall of one inch (2.5 cm) per hour is not uncommon, and a hurricane may produce a deluge of up to 22 billion tons (20 billion metric tons) of water a day. The change of water from vapor to liquid within a hurricane generates enormous amounts of energy: about 2,000 billion kilowatt hours per day, or enough to power the United States for a year.

When hurricanes reach land, their massive winds push water onto the shore, creating a **storm surge**. Category 4 and 5 hurricanes can generate storm surges of 20 to 25 feet (7.0 to 7.6 m) for a distance of 50 to 100 miles (80 to 160 km). The categories of hurricanes are outlined in the table on page 70. Giant waves,

Hurricane Rita, one of the massive storms that struck the United States in 2005, seen in a satellite photograph. *(NASA)*

up to 50 feet (15 m) high, ride atop a storm surge and cause even greater damage. If this potent combination strikes during a high tide, water rises even more. Where there is little elevation—such as the Atlantic and Gulf Coasts of the United States, which rise less than 10 feet (3 m) above sea level—flooding may reach far inland. Damage from Hurricane Camille in 1969, which hit land as a Category 5 hurricane, came primarily from the 24 foot (7.3 m) high storm surge that traveled as far as 125 miles (200 km) inland and damaged 18,000 homes.

Hurricanes move with the prevailing winds. In the North Atlantic and North Pacific, they originate in the trade winds and move toward the northwest. Once they are far enough north, they become trapped by the westerly winds and shift direction to the north or northeast. Hurricanes typically travel from 3 to 25 miles (5 to 40 km) per hour and can cover more than 500 miles (800 km) per day. Because their speed and direction are erratic—they can travel in a straight line, remain stationary, or make a loop—their course is not easily predicted.

Hurricanes typically last 5 to 10 days but may persist for up to three weeks. Once these mighty storms are cut off from warm water they lose strength, so they die fairly quickly when they move

The Saffir–Simpson Hurricane Scale

CATEGORY	MAXIMUM SUSTAINED WIND SPEED		DAMAGE
	(MPH)	(KPH)	
1 (weak)	74–95	119–153	Above normal; no real damage to structures
2 (moderate)	96–110	154–177	Some roofing, door, and window damage; considerable damage to vegetation, mobile homes, and piers
3 (strong)	111–130	178–209	Some buildings damaged; mobile homes destroyed
4 (very strong)	131–156	210–251	Complete roof failure on small residences; major erosion of beach areas; major damage to lower floors of structures
5 (devastating)	+156	+251	Complete roof failure on many residences and industrial buildings; some complete building failures

over cooler water or land. A strong, rapidly moving storm, though, can travel a long way before perishing, sometimes even moving quite far north and quite far inland. In September, 1938, a hurricane ravaged the region between Cape Hatteras, North Carolina, and New England, killing 600 and destroying 60,000 homes. The unnamed storm died only after passing over Montreal. When hurricanes weaken, they become unstable and produce intense rains and tornadoes.

Predicting a Hurricane's Path

Hurricanes are so deadly and so costly that, in recent years, all the relevant tools of modern science have been put to work studying them: satellites, airplanes, and super computers among others. One result of these efforts has been better predictions of where a hurricane is likely to go.

A forecast radar image map shows a wedge that grows wider with the distance from a storm's current location. A central line in the wedge shows the track that the storm is most likely to follow, but the storm may move anywhere within the wedge. While this can be frustrating to citizens who hope to learn the exact path of a storm, it gives the U.S. Navy and federal and local government services some idea of how to plan for each storm. Although the predictions are not perfect, in the past much larger parts of an area would be alerted to an oncoming storm. Now, the warnings inconvenience a much smaller area.

To predict where a hurricane will go, forecasters look at features of the atmosphere, ocean, and land. Storms move around regions of high or low pressure, which act as steering forces. If these steering forces are present, predicting a storm's direction is relatively simple. Without steering forces, a hurricane may slow or stall, and forecasters have difficulty predicting where it will go and when.

The Coming Storms

On average, the Atlantic spawns six hurricanes and many smaller tropical storms each year. In a five-year period, an average of three hurricanes strikes the U.S. coastline. However, these averages are not expected to remain the same in the coming decades. Since 1995, conditions have become much more favorable for the generation and maintenance of large hurricanes. The Atlantic north of the equator is now warmer, and wind shear between the lower and upper atmosphere has dropped. Scientists predict that this period of high hurricane intensity will last 10 to 40 years, likely for the longer term. When the same conditions reigned from the 1920s through the 1960s, there were many more storms than in the quiet period between 1971 and 1994,

Hurricane Katrina

The most destructive hurricane to hit the United States in historic times was born unceremoniously as Tropical Depression Twelve over the southeastern Bahamas on August 23, 2005. By the next morning, it had become Tropical Storm Katrina, and one day later it was a hurricane. That same day, the storm moved over south Florida as a Category 1 hurricane, killing nine people and causing an estimated $600 million in damage.

But that was just Katrina's opening act. The storm traveled west over the Gulf of Mexico, where water temperatures were as high as 89°F (32°C), providing ample heat for the storm to grow into a behemoth. On August 27, Katrina was upgraded to Category 3 and within just 24 hours it reached Category 5 with maximum sustained winds of 175 mph (280 kph) and gusts of 215 mph (344 kph). As the storm lumbered through the Gulf, Ray Nagin, the mayor of New Orleans, Louisiana, ordered an unprecedented mandatory evacuation of the city.

At 1:30 A.M., Monday, August 29, Hurricane Katrina made landfall as a Category 4 hurricane with peak winds of approximately 150 mph (240 kph). Its minimum pressure of 918 millibars (mbar) made it the third strongest hurricane to strike the United States. Although the storm had been headed straight for New Orleans, it veered slightly eastward as it neared the Gulf Coast, so that the city was struck by the less powerful, western eye wall of the storm. While New Orleans was spared the most intense winds and highest storm surge, the entire Gulf Coast, including Louisiana,

Hurricane Katrina seen from above. *(NASA /Jeff Schmaltz, MODIS Land Rapid Response Team)*

Flooding in New Orleans in the aftermath of Hurricane Katrina. Lake Pontchartrain, at the top of the photo, is the source of the water. At the bottom, near the banks of the Mississippi River, is the relatively high ground that did not become submerged. *(Lawrence Ong, EO-1 Mission Science Office, NASA, GSFC)*

Mississippi, Alabama, and Florida, was damaged. The 30-foot (9 m) storm surge at Biloxi, Mississippi, was the highest ever observed in the United States, and enormous amounts of damage were done. Federal disaster declarations covered 90,000 square miles (233,000 km) of the United States, an area almost as large as the United Kingdom. Once on land and cut off from its power supply of warm ocean water, the massive storm rapidly lost strength and was downgraded to a tropical depression within 24 hours.

News reports that New Orleans had been saved from the brunt of storm damage were premature. By late morning on August 29, the storm surge collapsed several sections of the levee system that kept water out of the city. Eventually, 80% of New Orleans would be underwater. Early on, Mayor Nagin estimated that there would be as many as 10,000 dead, but this number was nothing more than a guess. The actual death toll was around 1,300 in New Orleans alone, with as many as 2,500 fatalities in all. Additionally, one million people were displaced. As of early 2007, New Orleans is still a shambles, and many of its former residents are living their lives elsewhere.

when these conditions of warmer water and low wind shear did not predominate. But even quiet periods can have major hurricanes; one of the most devastating storms in history, Hurricane Andrew, struck in 1992. However, the predicted increase in hurricanes may be countered by another predicted atmospheric change—an increase in El Niño events. The weakening or reversal in the trade winds brought about by El Niño is thought by experts to suppress the formation and intensity of hurricanes.

In the five years between 1995 and 2000, hurricanes formed at a rate twice as great as during the quiet period between 1971 and 1994, with the Caribbean experiencing a five-fold increase. During this five-year period, the frequency of storms with sustained winds of more than 100 mph (160 km/hr) was 2.5 times as high. Wind speed is significant because a storm with 130 mph (209 km/hr) winds has almost double the strength of one with 100 mph (160 km/hr) winds. Indeed, even though they account for only one-fifth of the storms that make landfall, these intense 100-mph-plus storms produce more than 80% of the damage from all hurricanes put together.

Increases in the quantity and severity of hurricanes will have different consequences for different locations. In the United States, where there are good warning and social services systems, most of the greatest storm losses will be measured in property. The six major storms that struck the United States in 2004 caused damages of about $42 billion. In 2005, the more than $100 billion price tag from Hurricane Katrina dwarfed the previous record holder, Hurricane Andrew, whose damages totaled $36 billion (adjusted for inflation). Hurricane Katrina also showed that even a developed nation is not immune to high fatalities from storms. In the Caribbean, where social services are not as well developed, the loss of life from a severe hurricane may be extreme.

EXTREME HEAT

With far less drama than a storm, extreme heat kills more people in the United States than lightning, hurricanes, tornadoes, floods, and earthquakes combined. Only the cold of winter is responsible for more weather-related deaths. Health is impacted most when nighttime temperatures remain high and the heat does not abate for days, and when the high temperatures are coupled with high humidity.

To help people understand the dangers of heat coupled with humidity, the NWS has devised the **heat index** (HI). The HI was developed to assist people in making good choices about activity levels and exposure during the hottest summer days. To determine the HI on a given day, find the intersection of the measured temperature and the percent humidity in the table below. For example, the HI of a 95°F (35°C) day with 70% humidity is 122°F.

The health effects of that temperature are listed in the table on page 76; in this case, prolonged exposure or physical activity can lead to sunstroke, heat cramps, heat exhaustion, and heat stroke.

When the human body gets hot, it dissipates heat by evaporation during sweating, by varying the rate and depth of blood circulation, or even by panting. If the body's heat rises beyond its ability to cool, which is more common in the elderly, heat disorders develop. Heat stroke occurs when a body's core temperature rises to 105°F (40°C)

The Heat Index: Temperature (°F) or Temperature (°C) Coupled with Humidity (%)

T (°F)	T (°C)	90%	80%	70%	60%	50%	40%
80	26.7	85	84	82	81	80	79
85	29.4	101	96	92	90	86	84
90	32.2	121	113	105	99	94	90
95	35.0		133	122	113	105	98
100	37.8			142	129	118	109
105	40.6				148	133	121
110	43.3						135

Heat Index and Possible Heat Disorders

HEAT INDEX TEMPERATURE	POSSIBLE HEAT DISORDERS
80° F–90°F (26.6°C–32.2°C)	Fatigue possible with prolonged exposure and/or physical activity
90°F–105°F 32.2°C–40.6°C)	Sunstroke, heat cramps, and heat exhaustion possible with prolonged exposure and/or physical activity
105°F–130°F (40.6°C–54.4°C)	Sunstroke, heat cramps, and heat exhaustion likely and heat stroke possible with prolonged exposure and/or physical activity
130°F or greater (54.4°C or greater)	Heat stroke/sunstroke highly likely with continued exposure

Source: National Weather Service

or higher, resulting in organ damage and death. Sometimes a person succumbs to a heart attack that may have been triggered by stress due to excess heat. To calculate deaths from extreme heat, officials look at the number of deaths that occur above the normal rate for that period of time. Using this method, it was estimated that between 20,000 and 35,000 people—nearly 15,000 in France alone—died of heat-related problems in Western Europe in July and August 2003. Contributing to the problem of high temperatures was an increase in pollutants in the stagnant air.

DROUGHT

Drought is a change in the weather that is sustained over longer periods of time than either storms or excess heat. A region may be experiencing a drought if it has had a shortage of rainfall for days or weeks, or, more likely, for seasons or even years. The presence of a drought is determined by the distribution of precipitation over a given area before and during the dry period. Drought also is related to the effectiveness of any rains that fall. For example, if a region receives

The Dust Bowl

The Dust Bowl refers to areas of the American prairie—southeastern Colorado, southwestern Kansas, the Texas and Oklahoma panhandles, and northeastern New Mexico—that were devastated by drought in the 1930s. The region is characterized by cycles of rain and drought to which the native grasses are well adapted. During World War I, wheat prices were high due to the need to feed the Allied troops, and land that previously had been used for grazing was converted to farmland to meet demands. The native grasses that had held down the soil were plowed. This happened to be during a wet phase and the land, which had never been farmed before, was rich and fertile. As the rest of the country fell into the Great Depression, farms on the Great Plains thrived.

During this period, the land was over-cultivated and poorly managed. Then, in the summer of 1931, the rains stopped. In the years that followed, heavy winds lifted and blew away the topsoil that previously had been anchored by the native grasses that were now gone. Vast clouds of soil dust swept over the region. Thousands

A dust storm approaches a Kansas town in 1935. *(Historic NWS Collection)*

of families, comprising a quarter of the region's population, were forced from their land by these "black blizzards." In 1937, the federal government began to combat soil erosion with windbreaks and farming methods that prevented erosion, and much of the grassland was restored. In fall of 1938, the rains returned, and farmers could again make a living. Yet even with modern conservation measures and massive irrigation projects, some of the region's topsoil still blows away each year.

its entire annual rainfall in one quick storm, so that the water runs off the parched land and is unavailable for storage and use, the area still remains in drought.

Droughts affect humans far more than they affect other creatures. The organisms that live in arid regions are drought tolerant; they make use of water when it is available and live with little or none when it is not. For example, grasses that are native to the American Great Plains lie dormant during drought phases but can grow and reproduce tremendously during rainy periods. Humans trying to farm the region in the 1930s proved to be less flexible.

WRAP-UP

In the United States, the Midwest is dotted by springtime thunderstorms and tornados; the Southwestern deserts are blanketed by summer monsoon rains; the Gulf and Atlantic Coasts are struck regularly by hurricanes in summer and autumn; and the West has recurring droughts. Although these weather events are extreme, in relation to normal, day-to-day weather, they are still normal events. Even Category 4 and 5 hurricanes are normal, although they occur relatively infrequently. Fortunately, devastating storms like Hurricane Katrina are rare.

PART THREE

HUMAN INFLUENCE ON THE ATMOSPHERE: LOCAL IMPACTS

Air Pollutants
and Air Pollution

By far, most air pollution comes from the burning of fossil fuels. These pollutants can come directly from a smokestack or tailpipe, or they may be the result of a chemical reaction between these emissions and sunlight. Air pollutants include greenhouse gases, toxic gases, particulates, and compounds that react with water in the atmosphere to form acids, heavy metals, and ozone. The burning of forests and other plant materials produces similar pollutants. Another type of pollutant, volatile organic compounds (VOCs), enters the air mostly by evaporation. Some VOCs destroy the ozone layer, some are greenhouse gases, and some are toxic to the environment. Humans have been dealing with air pollution for millennia and have been restricting activities that foul the air for centuries. In the ongoing war of trying to keep air breathable, some battles are won and others are lost.

THE POLLUTANTS

Most medium and large cities around the globe are afflicted with air pollution. The table on page 82 lists the ten most polluted cities in

Most Polluted Cities in the United States, 2007

RANK	CITY	STATE
1	Los Angeles	California
2	Bakersfield	California
3	Visalia–Porterville	California
4	Fresno	California
5	Houston	Texas
6	Merced	California
7	Dallas–Fort Worth	Texas
8	Sacramento	California
9	New York	New York
10	Philadelphia	Pennsylvania

Source: American Lung Association

the United States in 2007. The ten most polluted cities in the world in 2006 were all in China, pushing Mexico City out of the top spot after it had spent decades as the world's most polluted city.

Although pollutants include constituents that are naturally part of the atmosphere, such as CO_2, human activities may release them in higher than normal quantities. Some compounds are pollutants because they are present in a region of the atmosphere where they do not belong; for example, the ozone that acts as a shield against UV rays in the stratosphere is a pollutant when it is in the troposphere. Other pollutants may cause important compounds that are naturally present to become less abundant, as with the destruction of stratospheric ozone by man-made chemicals. A few pollutants combine with water vapor to become acids. Excess heat also can be considered a pollutant, and urban areas suffer from increased temperatures and more variable weather as a result.

The Environmental Protection Agency (EPA) estimates that Americans put more than 160 million tons of air pollutants into the air in the United States each year. According to the EPA, in the United States, 49% of the air pollution is produced by transportation, 28% from fuel burned in factories and power planets, 13% from evaporation of volatiles, 3% from solid waste disposal, and 7% from miscellaneous other sources.

The EPA is required to control 189 air pollutants by the Clean Air Act, which is the law that sets standards for air quality in the United States. Six of these major pollutants—ozone, particulates, sulfur dioxide, nitrogen dioxide, carbon monoxide, and the heavy metal **lead**—are the primary focus of these regulations. Other important pollutants include benzene, found in gasoline; perchlorethlyene, emitted from some dry-cleaning facilities; and methylene chloride, used as a solvent and paint stripper. Dioxin, asbestos, toluene, and metals such as cadmium, mercury, chromium, and lead compounds also are included on the EPA's list. Some of these are discussed below.

POLLUTANTS FROM FOSSIL FUELS

Air pollution today is largely caused by the burning of fossil fuels. **Primary pollutants** enter the atmosphere directly, from a smokestack or tailpipe. **Secondary pollutants** form from a chemical reaction between a primary pollutant and some other component of air, such as water vapor or another pollutant. Ozone is the major secondary pollutant.

Fossil fuels come from decayed and transformed ancient organisms. Plants store CO_2 in their bodies, so plant materials that have been converted to fossil fuels emit CO_2 when burned. The two major types of fossil fuels are coal and petroleum. Coal forms in swamps, where plants grow and die in rapid succession. The plant bodies accumulate so quickly that little oxygen can get to them and they do not decay effectively. If this material is buried deeply enough, it is compressed and transformed into coal.

Petroleum forms in ocean regions, primarily along the margins of the continents, where **plankton**—tiny plants (phytoplankton) and animals (**zooplankton**)—flourish. When these organisms die, they fall to the sea floor and are buried by sediment. If they are buried deep enough, high temperatures and pressures convert them to oil and natural gas. Petroleum is a mixture of different hydrocarbons, which are compounds composed of hydrogen and carbon. When burned completely, these compounds produce CO_2 and water vapor. The energy that comes from burning fossil fuels can be thought of as ancient solar energy that was taken in by long-dead plants and animals.

The CO_2 and water vapor produced by the complete burning of pure coal and petroleum are both greenhouse gases. While greenhouse gases contribute to the warming of the Earth, which will be discussed in Chapter 14, they do not pose any direct threat to human health. But fossil fuels are rarely pure and often release other pollutants such as carbon monoxide (CO), nitrogen dioxide (NO_2), sulfur dioxide (SO_2), and hydrocarbons.

Carbon monoxide is a colorless, odorless gas that is lethal in high quantities. The EPA calls CO the "invisible" killer because it is undetectable. CO kills by substituting for O_2 in the blood, which starves the brain and other body parts of the much-needed O_2. In the United States, motor-vehicle exhaust accounts for about 60% of all CO emissions and as much as 95% of CO emissions in cities. Fortunately, emission-control devices have reduced CO levels by about 40% because the early 1970s. CO does not build without limit in the atmosphere, because it is removed by microorganisms in the soil. Nonetheless, this toxic gas causes problems in poorly ventilated tunnels or parking garages; because people cannot detect it by smell, it kills without warning. CO is a greenhouse gas.

The nitrous oxides (NO_x) are also greenhouse gases. Nitrifying bacteria in the soil and in plant roots naturally produce nitrous oxides during decomposition. These gases also are produced by human activities. When coal and petroleum are burned, they emit nitrogen, which reacts with O_2 to form NO_2 and NO. NO_2 is a noxious, reddish-brown gas that contributes to the mucky russet color and odor of the air in polluted cities. The concentration of NO_x in urban areas is 10 to 100 times greater than in rural areas. In wet air, NO_x reacts with H_2O to form nitric acid (HNO_3), a component of **acid rain**, which is rain that is considerably more acidic than normal rainwater.

Another major component of acid rain is sulfuric acid (H_2SO_4), which forms when sulfur dioxide (SO_2) mixes with water vapor (H_2O). SO_2, a common emission of low-grade coal and petroleum combustion, is a main ingredient of industrial pollution. When sulfur from burning impure coal reaches the air, it combines with oxygen to form sulfur oxides, mainly sulfur dioxide (SO_2) and sulfur trioxide (SO_3).

Mercury is a heavy metal that is released by burning coal, municipal and medical wastes, and by volcanic processes. According to the EPA, mercury is the most hazardous material emitted by power plants. The dangers of mercury have been known since the 1700s, when mercury salts were used to make fancy felt hats. Hatmakers who handled mercury-soaked fabric each day eventually would develop symptoms of uncontrollable twitching and trembling, due to mercury poisoning. This misunderstood condition inspired the phrase "mad as a hatter." Lewis Carroll used this image to create the character of the "Mad Hatter" for his children's book, *Alice's Adventures in Wonderland*.

As the story of the hatmakers illustrates, mercury does not do its damage as a gas. Although it is released into the air by combustion, it turns into aerosol droplets as it cools. These droplets can travel hundreds of miles through the atmosphere before falling to the ground or into the water, where they are deposited in sediments. Bacteria in the sediments then convert the droplets to organic mercury, usually the dangerous compound methyl mercury. When an organism takes in methyl mercury, the substance is stored in fat and muscle instead of being excreted. This means that animals accumulate all the methyl mercury that is contained in all the organisms that they eat. During their lifetimes, small organisms take in only a small amount of methyl mercury, but large, predatory animals, such as tuna and polar bears, eat more and store more of the substance. This process is called

bioaccumulation. Because of it, predatory fish that live at the top of the food chain, such as tuna, may have extremely high methyl mercury concentrations. This is a great risk to the birds, mammals, and humans that eat food that is located high on the food chain. (By contrast, aspirin does not bioaccumulate. A person can take the recommended dose of aspirin each day with no cumulative effect. Taking a daily dose of mercury would result in neurological problems and eventually death.)

Lead is the most common toxic material found in humans and enormous amounts of it are produced each year. Tetraethyl lead (a compound in which lead is combined with carbon and hydrogen) was first included as an ingredient in gasoline in the 1920s to increase fuel efficiency and to counter engine knock; it was also an ingredient in paints and other materials. Even when it was first used, tetraethyl lead was known to be toxic, but safer compounds were more expensive. In industrialized nations, lead has been banned from many uses, including gasoline, although it is still used in diesel fuels. The largest source of lead poisoning in the United States is in poor neighborhoods where children live with old, peeling lead paint.

POLLUTANTS FROM SECONDARY CHEMICAL REACTIONS

Some pollutants, most importantly ozone (O_3), do not come directly from fossil-fuel combustion but are the result of a two-step process. First, hydrocarbons from incompletely burned gasoline react with nitrogen oxides and atmospheric oxygen to form ozone. Second, the ozone reacts with automobile exhaust to form photochemical smog. These chemical reactions only occur in the presence of sunlight, so ozone pollution is at its worst on the sunny summer days common in places such as Southern California, southern Arizona, and Texas. Tropospheric ozone produces a white haze that sits over arid, car-dependent cities, most notably Los Angeles, California. This noxious, bad-smelling gas damages the lungs and is extremely harmful to animals and plants. Ozone is also a greenhouse gas.

As a secondary pollutant, ozone production can be decreased only if both nitrogen oxides and hydrocarbons are reduced. Therefore, it is a difficult problem to combat. Ozone is not restricted to cities; it also is produced in the countryside, where hydrocarbons are given off by vegetation, and nitrogen oxide pollution drifts out from urban areas to add to it.

POLLUTANTS FROM BIOMASS BURNING

Burning plant and animal material also produces pollutants. **Biomass** is the amount of living material found in an environment; in this case, material primarily from plants. **Slash-and-burn agriculture**, the preferred method for farming in tropical regions, is an enormous source of pollutants. In this type of agriculture, rain forests are chopped down and burned, and the land is then farmed. But rain forest soil is infertile and in a few years the farmer needs to slash and burn another patch of forest. Other biomass that is commonly burned includes savanna, fuel wood, leftover material from crops, and dried dung, which is burned for fuel.

The pollutants that are emitted from biomass burning are similar to those emitted by fossil fuels, because fossil fuels are ancient, transformed plant materials. As forests are razed, acrid smoke spreads far, instigating air pollution problems in neighboring countries, especially in Southeast Asia. Of primary concern are CO_2, CO, methane, particulates, nitrogen oxide, hydrocarbons, and organic and elemental carbon. The first three are greenhouse gases. Burning forests increases atmospheric CO_2 levels in two ways: by releasing the CO_2 that had been stored in the plants into the air, and by stopping the forest from sequestering more CO_2.

Particulates are the byproducts of fossil-fuel and biomass burning. They also can enter the atmosphere from natural sources such as volcanic ash or windblown dust. Most particulates are nontoxic, but they may cause health problems if they penetrate the lungs. Because particulates reduce visibility, they are the most noticeable air pollutants. Wind carries particulates great distances; for example, particulates from Europe cause the haze that coats the Arctic each spring. Particulates serve as nuclei for drops of snow, rain, or ice so their abundance has the potential to affect climate. Industrial processes generate nearly 40% of the estimated 15 billion pounds (6.6 million metric tons) of particulates emitted over the United States each year; vehicles create about 17% of particulate emissions.

VOLATILE ORGANIC COMPOUNDS

Volatile organic compounds (VOCs) are mostly hydrocarbons that enter the atmosphere primarily by evaporation. The EPA estimates that 18 million tons (16 million metric tons) of VOCs enter the atmosphere in the United States each year. Some VOCs form naturally, but most are synthetic (man-made). VOCs are found in paint thinners, dry-cleaning solvents, petroleum fuels, and wood preservatives, among other materials. There are tens of thousands of different VOCs in the air: Some are harmless, others are poisonous, and the effects of many are not fully known. Between 50 and 100 airborne VOCs are typically monitored. Methane (CH_4) is the most common VOC; it poses no immediate threat to human health, but it is a greenhouse gas. Although methane is produced naturally, it now enters the atmosphere in unnatural amounts due to an increase in certain agricultural practices. Some VOCs contribute to ozone production in the lower atmosphere.

Chlorofluorocarbons (CFCs) are synthetic VOCs. Although they were once widely used, they are now being phased out. These compounds are extremely stable. Long after their manufacture, they continue to rise into the upper atmosphere, where they break down stratospheric ozone. CFCs will eventually break apart and will no longer be able to destroy the ozone layer. CFCs are also greenhouse gases.

Some pollutants are compounds that are not manufactured or used; they are simply a byproduct of another process. The most important example is **dioxin**, which serves no useful purpose but is widespread in the environment. Dioxin is a byproduct of the production of herbicides, disinfectants, and other chemicals. This chemical also forms when specific compounds are burned, such as the plastic polyvinyl chloride. In this instance, some of the chlorine reacts with organic compounds to form dioxin. No living creature, no matter how remote its home, is completely untainted by dioxin. The harmful effects of dioxin are not yet fully understood, but it may restrict the body's ability to manufacture proteins and decrease immune system function. Some studies suggest that dioxin may cause **cancer**—the family of illnesses characterized by uncontrolled cell growth—and other serious illnesses.

THE HISTORY OF AIR POLLUTION AND AIR POLLUTION LEGISLATION

The burning of wood and coal for warmth and energy has caused problems for centuries, or even millennia. Ever since early humans made wood fires in their caves, people have been choking on the air. In 1306, King Edward I of England banned the use of sea coal, which produced acrid smoke, in London. The air in the city was so bad in 1661 that John Evelyn, the English author, wrote in *Fumifugium*, (one of the earliest books written about pollution problems), "That this Glorious and Ancient City . . . should wrap her stately head in clouds of smoke and sulphur, so full of stink and darkness, I deplore with just indignation."

In the 1850s, the term **smog** was coined for the combination of coal smoke and fog that regularly descended on London. The London fog was considered a symbol of power, mystery, and prosperity, despite the tens of thousands of Londoners who were afflicted with lung damage and rickets (due to the lack of sunlight). Smog was blamed for 700 deaths in 1873—19 of them people who accidentally walked into the Thames River because visibility was so poor—and 1,150 deaths in 1911. The worst event, called the "Big Smoke," came in early December 1952, when a thermal inversion and a stationary weather front calmed the winds to zero. All over London, the smog became so thick that visibility was reduced to nothing and pedestrians walking down the sidewalk had to feel their way along the outside walls of buildings.

Although many wore masks over their mouths, 4,000 people died over a period of five days. Twice as many others may have died over the next two months from influenza and other illnesses exacerbated by lung damage from the smog. Many of the fatalities occurred in adults who had chronic heart or lung disease, although infant mortality was twice the normal rate. This dire event prompted Parliament to pass a Clean Air Act in 1956 and, as a result, London's air is now much cleaner.

London's affliction was industrial smog, which pours through the smokestacks of coal- and heavy oil-burning factories. Cities in the United States have suffered similar difficulties; Chicago and Cincinnati passed their first clean air legislation in 1881. In the 1940s, the air above some coal-producing eastern U.S. cities became so laden with coal smoke that automobile headlights had to be turned on during the day. The turning point came in late October 1948, when coal smoke became trapped in the river valley where Donora, Pennsylvania, was located; 20 people died, and over 7,000—half of the town's population—were hospitalized or became ill. It was the first time U.S. officials recognized the relationship between smog and public health. This, and other incidents, led to passage of the federal Air Pollution Control Act of 1955, although its purpose was primarily to raise public awareness of the problem, and the act had little muscle. After its passage, pollution levels continued to be extremely high, with several severe events in the 1960s in New York City. In 1963, the first federal Clean Air Act was passed to reduce pollution from stationary sources, such as steel mills and power plants.

While the hazards of industrial pollution had been recognized for decades, photochemical smog was discovered in Southern California only in 1953. The first smog alert in Los Angeles occurred toward the end of World War II, and the problem continued to increase as the population of the area and number of vehicles grew. The first air pollution control agency in the area asked Arie Haagen-Smit, a plant biologist at the California Institute of Technology in Pasadena, California, to determine the source of the smog. Dr. Haagen-Smit, who had been using ozone as a tool to study pineapple scent, was the first to discover the chemical reaction that creates photochemical smog. Dr. Haagen-

Smit discovered that the sources of the raw material for photochemical smog were primarily cars and oil refineries and that the smog was a toxic soup that consisted of about 100 compounds. Although Haagen-Smit had intended to return to the study of pineapples, the condemnation he received from transportation-industry scientists spurred him to change his field of study to pollution science. He later became the first head of California's Air Resources Board.

The growing air pollution problems in Los Angeles, New York, and other cities led to the passage of the Clean Air Act of 1970. This law established primary and secondary standards for ambient air quality, set limits on emissions from stationary and mobile sources, empowered state and federal governments to enforce the law, and increased funding for air pollution research. The act was updated in 1990 to make emission requirements stricter. The Clean Air Act now regulates 189 toxic air pollutants and alternative fuels, and also monitors the pollutants that contribute to acid rain and stratospheric ozone depletion.

WRAP-UP

It is easy to see how early humans who gathered around fires for warmth and safety would have been unconcerned about the effect of the smoke on the environment around them. The atmosphere was vast and the smoke dissipated easily. It is even possible to see how people early in the twentieth century would see the emissions from car tailpipes as harmless and insignificant. Now, with more than six billion people on the planet, the atmosphere is being assaulted by a myriad of human activities, abundant in type and enormous in number. Air pollution is a huge and growing problem that requires legislation to combat. Unchecked, air pollutants have a variety of effects, from raising global temperature, to destroying natural atmospheric processes, to simply dirtying the air.

Air Pollution and the Environment

Air quality not only depends on the types and amounts of pollutants that are in the air, but also on external factors such as wind speed, atmospheric stability, and landscape. Stagnant air, such as the air beneath a temperature inversion or in a windless location, will collect more pollutants because clean air is not coming in, and pollutants are not being removed. Pollutants have an adverse effect on the environment. Particulates reduce visibility and obscure sunlight. Ozone alters the plant species found in an ecosystem and reduces crop yields. Even in areas that have been set aside for protection, such as national parks, air pollution can impact the natural system and the visitor experience.

EXTERNAL FACTORS THAT AFFECT AIR QUALITY

The amount and type of pollutants entering the air varies by time and location. Bad air days can occur in the winter, when there is a buildup of wood smoke or a temperature inversion, or in the summer, when photochemical smog is at its worst. The air quality of a location also depends on external features, such as winds, temperature inversions, and the local **topography** (the ups-and-downs of the landscape). Winds move polluted air away from a region or bring in fresh air to dilute it. On days when winds are strong, the air is rapidly cleansed. When there is little or no wind, the air stagnates, with little input of clean air and little chance for output of pollutants.

Temperature inversions trap cool air beneath warm air so that the cool air cannot rise. This puts a lid on the atmosphere so that anything that enters that volume of air is captured in it. The severity of the pollution depends on the height of the inversion. If the inversion is low, there is little air for mixing and pollution can reach dangerous levels. If the inversion is high, there is more air for mixing and the pollutants

Photochemical smog trapped beneath an inversion over Los Angeles, 1999. The view is northward toward smog-enshrouded downtown Los Angeles, with the Hollywood Hills in the background. *(Steve Smith / SuperStock)*

are diluted. Virtually any city can experience a temperature inversion; Los Angeles and New York are just two of them.

The topography of a region can contribute to its air quality. For example, a city located in a valley collects more pollutants than one that is located on a flat plain. Topography can also aid in changing pollution conditions both daily and seasonally. On cold winter nights, air sinks into valleys, forming an inversion and collecting pollutants. In the daytime, including during the summer season, the hills around valleys are heated by the Sun. During these periods, the air rises and pollutants cannot collect. This is why inversions are common in mountain valleys in the winter but not in the summer. Mountains also block winds, so air on the leeward side of a mountain range may stagnate and collect pollutants. Los Angeles is a good example of a city in which the topography couples with the large quantity of pollutant emissions to create a very smoggy city.

THE EFFECTS OF PARTICULATES ON THE ENVIRONMENT

Particulates primarily affect the environment by impairing visibility, reducing solar radiation, and altering climate. Particulates impair visibility in large cities, small towns where there is a lot of industry, and even in the national parks. The natural range of visibility in the United States is approximately 45 to 90 miles (75 to 150 km) in the East and 120 to 180 miles (200 to 300 km) in the West, but visibility in both regions has decreased to about one-half to two-thirds of normal in the western United States and about one-fifth of normal in the eastern United States. The National Park Service (NPS) has found that air pollution currently impairs visibility in many national parks across the country.

Particulates also reduce the quantity and quality of radiation received by plants, sometimes obstructing photosynthesis. Particulates can alter climate by changing temperature and precipitation; increase nutrients, such as nitrogen and iron; and cause acid rain. Some of these

Why Is Los Angeles So Smoggy?

The city of Los Angeles is legendary for its smog. On its worst day, in the summer of 1955, downtown Los Angeles suffered through hourly average ozone levels that were six times the amount allowable under current federal regulations. Summer days in the 1970s are remembered for the orange pall that obscured everything. Dr. Catherine Propper, a biologist at Northern Arizona University, grew up in the San Fernando Valley, most of which is within the City of Los Angeles. In a 2006 interview, she described her experiences: "I rode horses next to the mountains to the north, but on many days you wouldn't know that a range rose above 8,000 feet directly above the ranch because the pollution was so thick. On those days, I'd go home after riding and spend the rest of my day recuperating on the couch, concentrating on not taking deep breaths because it was simply too painful."

Since the early 1970s, California has made great strides in controlling air pollution. Yet, despite many triumphs, Los Angeles still has the most polluted air in the country. In his 2005 book *War Reporting for Cowards* author Chris Ayres describes the city's current pollution as "the rim of smog lining the horizon like scum on an unwashed sink."

There is a confluence of reasons for the severity of smog in the Los Angeles Basin: There are many pollution sources, and the environmental conditions are favor-

(continues)

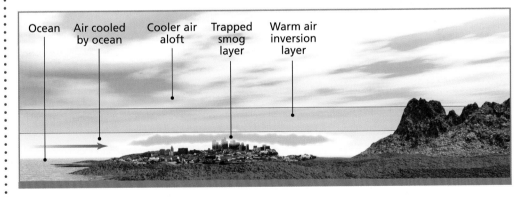

Ocean | Air cooled by ocean | Cooler air aloft | Trapped smog layer | Warm air inversion layer

A thermal inversion in which cool air from the ocean is trapped beneath warm air above, allowing the stagnant air above the city to collect pollutants. This illustration shows a common situation above Los Angeles.

(continues)

able for producing and trapping smog. Los Angeles is a sprawling metropolis. People spend many hours in their cars, which are the major pollution source. Between May 1 and October 1, when the famous Southern California sunshine streams down, photochemical smog is rampant. Southern California is also home to many oil refineries, which turn crude oil into useful substances such as gasoline, grease, and chemicals for plastics, nylon, and pesticides while contributing more pollution. In addition, the Los Angeles Basin is surrounded by the Pacific Ocean on the west and small and large mountain ranges to the north, east, and south. When the air over the land becomes warm and rises, cool air from over the Pacific moves inland. This creates an inversion that is nearly unremitting in the summer months. Trapped air collects pollutants that remain for days or weeks because there is little mixing or dilution by wind.

effects may inhibit plant growth and some may increase it. Deviation from natural conditions may favor nonnative species so that an ecosystem will be overrun with species that do not belong within it.

THE EFFECTS OF OZONE ON THE ENVIRONMENT

Ozone affects trees and other natural plants and food crops. Commonly, ozone slows plant growth rates. Food crops vary in their sensitivity to the gas; some are affected a great deal and some not at all. Spinach, for example, develops spotted leaves, which make it unmarketable; soybeans suffer reduced crop yields. Different amounts of ozone damage occur under different environmental conditions. Ozone enters plants through small openings in their leaves known as the **stoma**. Conditions that cause the stoma to open more, such as strong light or high temperature and humidity, maximize ozone damage to the plant. Conditions that cause the stoma to close, such as a shortage of water or the presence of some pollutants, lessen the damage. Developing nations, such as India and China, are particularly vulnerable to crop loss due to ozone pollution since they need to maximize food production and are also likely to have serious air pollution problems. Because the effects of ozone on crop plants are lessened by increased CO_2, and because atmospheric CO_2 is increasing, it is possible that the broader consequences of ozone pollution are not yet being realized.

Ozone may also alter natural ecosystems. Forests are especially vulnerable since trees live a long time and ozone effects accumulate over many years. Some trees are more sensitive to ozone than others, and if a forest's native trees become sick or die, they may be replaced by more ozone-tolerant species. Tree species that are sensitive to ozone include American sycamore (*Platanus occidentalis*), flowering dogwood (*Cornus florida*), Jeffrey pine (*Pinus jeffreyi*), paper birch (*Betula papyrifera*), quaking aspen (*Populus tremuloides*), red maple (*Acer rubrum*), and white pine (*Pinus strobus*). If ozone damage becomes too great, these important species may be lost and nonnative species may move into forest areas. With different trees forming the forest framework, entire ecosystems can be altered.

Other pollutants besides particulates and ozone cause damage to the environment. Nitrogen oxides and sulfur oxides in the atmosphere create acids that fall as acid rain. Toxic pollutants, such as metals and VOCs, can bioaccumulate, causing harm to animals—including people—who are high on the food chain.

AIR POLLUTION AND THE NATIONAL PARKS

The national parks are a good place to gain understanding of the effects of air pollution on the environment. The parks are small and contained, and many have been well studied over many decades. Although national parks are set aside from the rest of the landscape, they do not exist in isolation: Traffic, noise, and air and water pollution invade them no matter where they are. Most air pollution in national parks comes from outside park boundaries, and some of the greatest jewels of the park system are positioned near urban areas, power plants, and industrial complexes.

Shenandoah National Park, located in Virginia, is near a well-developed region. The park straddles a beautiful section of the Blue

Ridge Mountains, delighting its visitors with cool forests, deep canyons, lovely waterfalls, and expansive views of the rugged landscape. In 1886, those views inspired naturalist George Freeman Pollock to write, "To say that I was carried away is to put it mildly. I raved, I shouted." Since then, the average summer visibility has dropped from 90 miles (145 km) to less than 20 miles (30 km). Winds bring in coal smoke from an expanding number of coal-fired power plants in Virginia and the Ohio Valley. Once inside park boundaries, the pollutants are trapped by the tall mountains and deep valleys. At times, the smog in the Shenandoah is worse than in some major industrial cities.

Shenandoah National Park is designated as deserving of the highest protection afforded by the Clean Air Act. Since the act's passage, visibility has improved, but the situation is still bad. In 1996, only 31% of summer days had "good" visibility of over 30 miles (50 km). Ozone levels are high enough that sensitive plants are being injured;

Shenandoah National Park has much lower visibility than it once did. *(David R. Frazier / Photo Researchers)*

weakened plants are more vulnerable to other problems such as invasions by insects. The ozone is so bad that health standards are being violated. Adverse health effects from air pollution are possible on employees and park visitors.

Some parks are far removed from development, yet they are still polluted. This is true of Yellowstone National Park, where the primary source of pollution is park visitors. In the winter, snowmobiles emit toxic air pollutants, such as the VOCs benzene and toluene, plus CO and methane. Winter inversions trap pollutants, further impacting air quality. Substantial air pollution levels have been measured, even in remote park locations. Summer days are not pollutant-free either; cars and motor homes create ground-level ozone and other air pollutants.

Some national parks endure pollution from both inside and outside their boundaries. The most popular destination in Yosemite National Park in California is the majestic Yosemite Valley, where granite domes and cliffs carved by glaciers are adorned with cascading waterfalls. Yet, on summer weekends, visitors jam thousands of cars and motor homes into the valley's small space, which becomes filled with smoke from campfires and the occasional wildfire. Yosemite lies adjacent to California's San Joaquin Valley, which contains tremendous sources of agricultural and motor vehicle pollution. Pesticides and other chemicals from the San Joaquin Valley waft into the park, causing problems for aquatic and terrestrial organisms. Ozone damages plant species, including the unique and important ponderosa pine (*Pinus ponderosa*). Nitrogen pollutants injure the native plants that have evolved under nitrogen-poor conditions and favors nonnative, nitrogen-tolerant species. Visibility in the park suffers; even in the photo of Half Dome on the National Park Service brochure, the mountain seems to be mired in haze.

WRAP-UP

Air pollution damages the environment by harming plants and obscuring views, among other effects. Some locations are more impacted, such as those that are highly developed or near development and those that have a topography that traps air for long periods. National parks illustrate the effects of pollution on the environment. Air pollution weakens plants and makes them more vulnerable to other stresses, such as disease, insect infestation, or drought. Native plant species are driven out and replaced by nonnatives, causing the entire ecosystem to be altered. Even the human experience is compromised; air pollution mires beautiful vistas in haze and may result in adverse health effects.

Air Pollution
and Human Health

More than 120 million Americans live in areas where the air is unhealthy. For some, the serious effects amount to nothing more than itchy eyes or the need to curtail outdoor activities. But for many, particularly children, the elderly, and people with other health conditions, air pollution can cause debilitating illnesses or hasten death. While the costs of keeping down pollution levels are high, the costs of not keeping them down are even higher.

WHO IS AT RISK?

Not all people are equally at risk for health problems from air pollution. Children are vulnerable because their lungs are growing and developing; they also have a larger lung-surface area per unit body weight, so they take in 50% more air per unit body weight than adults. For example, infants have up to eight times the amount of ozone entering the deep portions of their lungs compared to adults. Children are also less able to fight off illnesses because of their developing immune systems. In addition, young people spend more time outdoors than adults, particularly in the summer when ozone levels are high. When children exercise or play, they take in more air, which increases their exposure to pollutants. If lung growth and function are harmed, the child may develop respiratory-tract illnesses or even long-term lung damage.

The elderly are also at increased risk for health problems from air pollution, which may exacerbate the health problems they already have. People of any age who have chronic health problems, such as asthma and heart and lung disease, are also more susceptible to the effects of air pollution. For example, people with type 2 diabetes are at higher risk for cardiovascular troubles if they ingest airborne particles.

HEALTH EFFECTS OF AIR POLLUTION

Most of the effects people experience from air pollution are short term: irritation to the eyes, nose, and throat; headaches; nausea; allergic reactions; or upper respiratory infections, such as bronchitis and pneumonia. But short-term problems depend not only on the duration of exposure, but also on the concentration of exposure, as seen during the "Big Smoke" in London in 1952, when 4,000 people died after just a few days of high exposure. Most air-quality standards were developed for average exposures that rise and fall depending on emissions and on environmental conditions. However, the average air quality has continued to decline, causing many people to have more days of exposure to poor air over time.

The long-term health effects of smog can also be dramatic. There is no specific "air pollution disease" but exposure to air pollution may cause chronic respiratory disease, heart disease, and damage to the brain, nerves, liver, or kidneys, or even premature death. The Environmental Science Engineering Program at the Harvard School of Public Health in a 2002 report concluded that approximately 4% of the death rate in the United States can be attributed to air pollution. People exposed to sufficient concentrations of toxic air pollutants over long enough time periods have an increased chance of contracting lung and other cancers. Other health effects include decreased immune system function and reduced fertility. The major pollutants and their health effects are listed in the table below.

Health Consequences of the Six Major Air Pollutants

POLLUTANT	EFFECTS
Ozone	Irritates respiratory system, reduces lung function, aggravates asthma, damages the cells lining the lungs, aggravates chronic lung disease, causes permanent lung damage in children
Particulates	Aggravate asthma and other respiratory illnesses, may cause chronic bronchitis, decrease lung function, bring about premature death
Sulfur oxides	Intensify asthma and other respiratory disease, cause respiratory illnesses, bring about difficulty in breathing and premature death
Nitrogen oxides	Irritate respiratory system, aggravate respiratory conditions such as asthma and chronic bronchitis
Carbon monoxide	Reduces oxygen delivery to organs and tissues; exacerbates cardiovascular disease; brings about visual impairment, reduced work capacity, reduced manual dexterity, poor learning ability, difficulty performing tasks; can be poisonous at high concentrations
Lead	Brings about gastrointestinal pain, nervous system damage, and encephalitis; chronic exposure can lead to brain, kidney, nervous system, or red blood cell damage; children can experience lowered intelligence and visual-motor problems

Particulates and ozone seem to do the most damage. Fine particles pose the greatest health risks since they penetrate the lung's natural defense mechanisms. The Natural Resources Defense Council estimates that 64,000 premature deaths from cardiopulmonary (heart and lung) illnesses may be attributable to particulate pollution each year. Abt Associates, a research firm located in Cambridge, Massachusetts, conducted a study in 2000 that looked at the health effects of particle pollution emitted from power plants alone. The study concluded that each year more than 30,000 deaths and more than 603,000 asthma attacks are attributable to fine-particle pollution. For asthma, traffic pollution—particularly from trucks—is an even worse offender. Sulfur and nitrogen oxides impair lung function and exacerbate diseases such as asthma and emphysema. These gases affect the heart and liver and increase vulnerability to viral infections such as the flu. Ozone irritates the respiratory system, causing problems with lung function. The gas increases susceptibility to heart disease and cancer in some people. The following sections discuss some of the more common and harmful illnesses caused by air pollution.

METAL POISONING

Toxic metals cause serious problems in humans, especially in children. One example is mercury. Fossil fuel burning releases the metal into the environment, and people ingest it when they eat large predatory fish, such as tuna, in which it has bioaccumulated. Methyl mercury enters the body's cells, causing nervous system and brain damage, including loss of motor control, limb numbness, blindness, and loss of ability to speak. Mercury poisoning is irreversible.

Elevated mercury levels that are not high enough to cause problems in an adult may cause problems in a developing fetus or nursing infant since growing bodies are far more easily damaged than adult ones. In children, mercury poisoning shows up as brain or developmental damage, learning disabilities or reduced cognitive ability, and problems with motor skills such as walking, talking, or hand-eye coordination. A 2005 study by scientists at Mount Sinai Center for Children's Health and Environment in New York, New York, shows that between 316,000 and 637,000 American children experience reductions in intelligence each year due to mercury pollution. This will ultimately result in a loss of $8.7 billion in earnings annually, far more than the cost would be to reduce mercury output from industries. Of women of childbearing age in the United States, 21% have mercury levels that exceed EPA guidelines, and about 8% have blood mercury levels that could hurt brain development in a fetus. This puts about 600,000 American newborns at risk for mercury poisoning.

ASTHMA

Asthma, a chronic inflammatory respiratory disease characterized by periodic attacks of wheezing, shortness of breath, and a tight feeling in the chest, is the most visible health impact of dirty air. This chronic illness afflicts over 20.3 million Americans, 5.5 million of which are children. Between 1980 and 1995, the prevalence of asthma among children ages 5 to 14 in the United States increased 2.5 times. A survey of more than 13,000 students by the U.S. Centers for Disease Control and Prevention in 2005 found that one in six high school students suffers from asthma, and more than one-third of those had an attack in the previous year, making the disease one of the leading causes of school absenteeism. Even the youngest children are at risk for problems, with air pollution causing premature birth or death in some infants. Worldwide, there are 300 million asthma sufferers, and that figure is expected to jump to 400 million in 20 years according to participants at the 2004 World Asthma Meeting. In many countries, the prevalence of asthma is rising 20% to 50% every 10 years.

As with other diseases, developing asthma requires two factors: having genes that make a person susceptible to it, and being exposed to something critical in the environment. Children who are exposed to secondhand smoke or polluted outdoor or indoor air are especially vulnerable. For example, children living within 650 feet (200 m) of a busy street are more likely to develop asthma. Children who live near truck traffic, which emits large amounts of particulates, are also more vulnerable. Nearly two-thirds of asthmatics in the United States live in an area where at least one federal air-quality limit is exceeded, and studies have found an increase in the severity of asthma attacks during particularly polluted periods.

The biggest culprits for triggering asthma attacks and worsening the condition are O_3, SO_2, and particulates. Diesel-engine exhaust particles inflict more damage than other particulates. Asthma attacks are responsible for nearly 2 million visits to the emergency room and more than 4,000 deaths annually. The annual economic cost is enormous as well, estimated at $14 billion in 2002.

Setting up a study to look at the effects of air pollution and asthma would be impossible, but amazingly there are two cases in which this was done inadvertently. During the 1996 Olympic Games in Atlanta, the downtown was closed to private cars, public transit was easily available, and workers were encouraged to telecommute. These changes brought a 28% reduction in ozone levels, which was correlated with approximately a 40% decline in hospitalizations for asthma. In Utah County, Utah, there were 50% fewer hospital admissions of children for asthma and pneumonia during the winter when a strike closed the local steel mill, as compared with the winters before and after the strike. As the above may indicate, while asthma can not be cured, it may be controlled through reduction of pollutants.

LUNG CANCER

Cancer is not a single disease, but a group of more than 100 distinct diseases. The unifying trait of all cancers is the uncontrolled growth of abnormal cells in the body. Although treatments have been significantly improved in the past half century, cancer is the cause of one in every four deaths in the United States. More than 30% of the people who receive a cancer diagnosis from their doctor will be dead of the disorder within five years, although some cancers can be treated successfully.

Cancer can be caused by **carcinogens**, which are chemical or physical substances that can cause cells to grow uncontrollably. Chemical carcinogens include chemical emissions from industry; pollutants from cars, homes, and factories; and tobacco smoke. Physical carcinogens include UV radiation from sunlight and ionizing radiation from X-rays and radioactive materials. A number of viruses

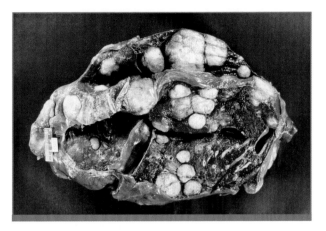

A human lung with cancer. *(Martin M. Rotker / Photo Researchers)*

can cause cancer, as can repeated local injury or recurring irritation to a part of the body. How carcinogenic a substance is depends, in part, on the dose a person receives. With enough exposure, some substances will cause cancer in almost anyone.

Lung cancer is the main respiratory cancer, and its primary cause is smoking. Studies have also found a strong link between the disease and long-term exposure to air pollution, primarily from fine particulates. A 2002 study by Brigham Young University, located in Provo, Utah, tracked 500,000 people in over 100 U.S. cities for 15 years and showed that the risk of a nonsmoker dying from lung cancer rose with increasing pollution and concluded that no level of air pollution could be considered safe. The study found that the long-term effects of breathing heavily polluted air are the same as breathing secondhand smoke. This is the reason that many private and public establishments no longer allow tobacco smoking on their premises. The study also found that the risk of dying from heart disease, or of dying from any cause, increased with higher air pollution levels. Diesel engines are responsible for 70% of California's cancer risk from air pollution, according to the Union of Concerned Scientists.

PREMATURE DEATHS

Premature deaths, from a variety of causes, can be attributed to air pollution. The World Health Organization estimates that bad air kills 600,000 people worldwide each year. Air pollution has also been linked to spontaneous abortions (miscarriages) and increased infant mortality. A 2000 study by the Ontario Medical Association, in Ontario, Canada, a city with about 12 million people, showed that air pollution causes approximately 2,000 premature deaths in that city annually. A 1999 study of 11 Canadian cities by the Canadian Air Health Effects Division found that approximately 5,000 preventable premature deaths (about 8% of the total) could be attributed to air pollutants. The study estimated that in 1995 the Greater Toronto area had experienced just slightly more deaths from lung cancer than from air pollution.

Surprisingly, long-term exposure to particulate matter in polluted air is more likely to cause death from cardiovascular disease than from respiratory problems. Particulates bring about inflammation, which accelerates **atherosclerosis** (the accumulation of fatty deposits in the arteries) and alters the ability of the heart to function. The Natural Resources Defense Council, with the assistance of scientists at the Harvard Medical School, estimated in 2002 that about 6.5% of all deaths in the United States from cardiopulmonary causes, which total 986,000 per year, are related to air pollution.

THE COSTS

Medical conditions arising from air pollution can be very expensive, costing billions of dollars in the United States each year. This includes health-care costs, lost worker productivity, and the impacts on human welfare. A cost-benefit analysis for Mexico City, with one of the worst air pollution problems in the world, estimated that a 10% reduction in air pollution below levels found in the late 1990s would lead to a decrease in health costs by roughly $2 billion per year. Reducing 75% of California's emissions of diesel particulates from year 2000 levels by 2010, and 85% by 2020, would save the state $48 billion to $70 billion between 2004 and 2020, according to the Union of Concerned Scientists. A nationwide strengthening of emission standards for heavy diesel equipment would prevent 9,600 premature deaths each year by 2030 and save the United States $81 billion in 2030.

WRAP-UP

The medical costs of air pollution are high, and they do not make up the entire price tag. Asthma and other pollution-related ailments decrease the quality of life for many people and reduce worker productivity. Although reducing pollution is expensive, these costs are often not weighed against the total costs that come from pollution, many of which have no dollar value. When all of these factors are taken into account, it is likely that the benefits to human health and the environment are well worth the costs of keeping down pollution.

Acid Rain

Acid rain is different from the other types of air pollution. For one thing, tailpipes and smokestacks do not emit acids; the acid rain forms from a combination of pollutants and water vapor in the atmosphere. Acid rain does not do its major damage in the atmosphere, but in lakes, ponds, and streams. Besides making surface waters more acidic, acid rain strips the soil of its nutrients, thus damaging trees by depleting their nurient supply as well as by harming their leaves and needles. Acid rain leaches metals from soil; the metals are then deposited near the top of the soil where they harm trees, or are carried into ponds, where they can hurt freshwater animals. Large amounts of acid rain change a pond's or a lake's ecosystem and in some cases may completely destroy it. This chapter will describe how acid rain forms and the consequences it has on the natural and even the cultural environment. It will also discuss effective strategies for decreasing acid rain formation and mitigating its effects.

WHAT IS ACID RAIN?

Acid rain is rain that is more acidic than normal; by definition, it has a **pH** of less than 5.0. The pH of a substance is a measure of its acidity or alkalinity. Natural rainfall is slightly acidic, with a pH of about 5.6. The acidity of natural rain is due to the small amount of CO_2 that dissolves in rainwater and forms mild carbonic acid.

There are several steps to the creation of acid rain. Sulfur dioxide (SO_2) and the nitrogen oxides (NO_x) are released during the combustion of coal and petroleum, or from the refining of metal ores. In the United States, about two-thirds of all SO_2 and one quarter of all NO_x come from electric power plants, which mostly burn coal for energy. The gases then react with water vapor in the air to produce sulfuric acid and nitric and nitrous acid. These acids

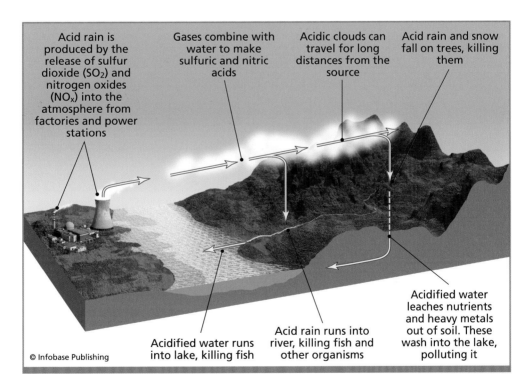

Sulfur compounds combine with water in the atmosphere to form sulfuric acid that eventually falls as acid rain.

Acidity and pH

Acidic substances, like lemons, have a sour taste. Strong acids can be harmful; for example, they may burn skin. The acidity of a substance is measured on the pH scale. The H in pH refers to the free positively charged hydrogen ions. The numbers of the pH scale range from 0 to 14, where 7 is neutral, meaning that the substance is neither acidic nor **alkaline**. Numbers higher than 7 are alkaline (also known as *basic*) and lower than 7 are acidic. The lowest numbers are the strongest acids, and the highest numbers are the strongest bases. The pH scale is logarithmic, so a change in one unit reflects a tenfold increase or decrease in acidity. Therefore, even small changes in pH mean large changes in acidity. If clean rain has a pH of 5.6, rain with a pH of 4.6 is ten times more acidic and rain with a pH of 3.6 is 100 times more acidic.

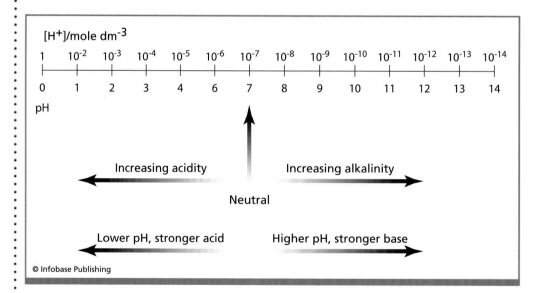

The pH scale. A neutral solution has a pH of 7.0; less than 7.0 is acidic and greater than 7.0 is alkaline. Hydrogen ion concentration is shown on the upper axis of the scale.

dissolve in water droplets, which fall as rain—in this case, acid rain.

Sulfuric and nitric acids are strong acids. Rainwater in the northeastern United States has 10 times the acidity of natural rain, typically with a pH between 4.0 and 4.5. This region is afflicted with highly acidic precipitation due to the high density of medium and large-sized industrial cities, such as Pittsburgh; the high population density of the interconnected cities and suburbs in the zone from Washington, D.C., north to Boston; and the concentration of power and industrial plants in West Virginia and other regions. In addition to the smog produced locally, acid-producing pollutants are blown in from the Midwest.

Acid rain is not the only form of precipitation that has a lower pH; any type of precipitation can be acidic and is called **acid precipitation**. For example, acid fog can do more damage than acid rain, since rain falls on the upper surface of an object, but fog surrounds an object. Acid fog, with an average pH of 3.4, is also more acidic than acid rain. Fog on a mountain can be 10 times more acidic than the rain falling nearby. An acidic fog in Southern California in 1986 had a pH of 1.7, nearly as acidic as toilet bowl cleaner. Part of the reason for the higher acidity of fog is that the small droplets have more surface area for pollutants to dissolve into. Acid particles may act as condensation nuclei, and the small droplets of acid fog will contain many more condensation nuclei than the larger droplets of acid rain. Acid snow, another form of acid precipitation, may lie on the ground for months, bringing a sudden rush of acid into lakes and streams during the spring thaw.

Acid deposition also can be dry, as it is in the arid Los Angeles area, where 12 times more nitric acid is deposited dry than in liquid precipitation. In dry deposition, acidic gases and particles simply settle to the ground or blow into buildings, cars, homes, and trees. Particles can then be washed from surfaces to join water that fell as acid rain, making the resulting mixture even more acidic.

Sulfur and nitrogen oxides released from tall smokestacks may drift as far as 600 miles (1,000 km) downwind (in the direction the wind is blowing), so the regions that experience acid rain problems may not be

A forest of spruce trees that has been devastated by acid rain. *(Simon Fraser / Photo Researchers)*

the regions where the pollutants originate. This situation has strained relations among states and nations. The Scandinavian countries, where acid rain is causing an environmental crisis, are in this predicament. All the rain that fell on Sweden in 2000, for example, had a pH of less than 5.05. Most of these emissions come from the factories of the United Kingdom and Western Europe. Fortunately, these countries have decreased their emissions by 70% since that time, and the rain's natural acid balance is slowly returning in Scandinavia. Canada's acid rain problem originates largely in the factories and power plants of the United States. In 1998, the United States produced more than six times the SO_2 emissions and 11 times the NO_x emissions of Canada.

Decreases of 40% of emissions in the United States have begun to be felt in Canada. However, rainfall is becoming increasingly acidic in Southeast Asia, where pollutant emissions are growing tremendously.

A BRIEF HISTORY OF ACID PRECIPITATION

Acid precipitation is not a new problem; it has simply become a bigger problem. The term *acid rain* was coined in 1856 by a British chemist named Robert Angus Smith who noticed that plants downwind of industrial areas, even in areas located a great distance from the source, were being damaged. In 1962, Swedish scientist Svante Odgen compiled records from the 1950s indicating that acid rain came from air masses moving out of Central and Western Europe into Scandinavia. In the late 1960s and early 1970s, scientists in Scandinavia and the United States who were monitoring rainwater, lakes, and streams found that pH values were decreasing. Initially, the problem in the United States was concentrated in the northeastern states of New York and Pennsylvania because the type of coal burned there was more sulfuric. By 1980, most of the states east of the Mississippi, as well as southeastern Canada, were receiving acidic rainfall, largely from coal burned in the midwestern United States. For the first time, acid rain was identified as a regional, rather than a local, problem. In the western United States, where much less coal is burned, acid rain primarily forms from tailpipe emissions from vehicles.

During the 1980s, a great deal of research was done on acid precipitation. Scientists uncovered the mechanics of acid rain formation and learned of the types of acid deposition. They monitored trends in the acid content of rain, lake, and stream water and observed the effects of acid rain on ecosystems and on historical and cultural structures. They described how acid precipitation might be controlled. The trend toward increasing acidity in water and its effects prompted the U.S. Congress to amend the Clean Air Act to control emissions of sulfur and nitrogen oxides in 1990. Canada and the nations of the European Union have also greatly reduced emissions in the past two decades.

THE EFFECTS OF ACID RAIN

Acid rain has little effect on some regions yet is very harmful in others. Besides the pH of the water, the local environment plays a role in how much damage acid precipitation can cause. Some materials, including some rock and soil, can neutralize an acidic or an alkaline solution, a quality called **buffering capacity**. Rocks and soils that contain calcium carbonate (sometimes called **lime**) are the best acid buffers. These include limestone, marble, and their soils. The pH of ponds and streams situated in those rock types will be nearly normal. Nebraska, Indiana, and other Midwestern states do not suffer from acid rain problems due to their well-buffered soils. Even in these locations, though, if the buffering capacity of a soil or rock is exceeded, the region will be vulnerable to acid damage.

Most rock and soil has little buffering capacity, so acidic waters can cause a great deal of damage. Materials with poor buffering capability include the metamorphic rocks of the northeastern United States. In these regions, some soils have increased their acid levels by five to ten times in the past few decades. Acidic soils lower the pH of streams that flow over them. According to the Environmental Protection Agency (EPA), in 2007 approximately 580 of the streams in the Mid-Atlantic Coastal Plain are acidic; this includes 90% of the streams in the Pine Barrens of New Jersey, the highest percentage in the nation. Acidic streams feed lakes, ponds, and marshes, which exacerbates the problem caused by acid rain. The combined acidity has lowered the pH of some lakes in the Northeastern United States to below 5.0; Little Echo Pond in Franklin, New York, has a pH of 4.2. The Canadian government estimates that 14,000 lakes in eastern Canada are acidic. In Sweden, 18,000 lakes are so acidic that all the fish have died.

Acid rain causes damage as it filters through soil. Hydrogen ions from the acid invade minerals in the soil and replace elements that are good plant nutrients, such as calcium, magnesium, and potassium. The freed nutrients are then washed away so the soil is no longer able to nourish plants. Acidic waters can also leach metals, such as aluminum, from the soil and transport them to freshwater lakes, ponds, and streams where they accumulate and may become toxic to fish.

ACID RAIN AND FRESHWATER ECOSYSTEMS

Water with low pH diminishes the quantity and variety of life in lakes and streams. Most aquatic plants grow best in water with a pH of 7.0 to 9.2. As pH decreases, populations of submerged aquatic plants decline, reducing food for some water birds. Numbers of freshwater shrimp, crayfish, clams, and some fish start to dwindle. At pH 5.5, the bacteria that decompose leaf litter and other debris begin to die, cutting off the supply of organic material for plankton. Aluminum leached from the soil by acidic water enters the lake in great quantities, putting fish populations under even more stress. Young fish hatching into acidic, metal-rich waters do not survive into adulthood, or they may be deformed or stunted in their growth. Females under stress will not spawn, and fish eggs will not hatch if the pH is less than 5. Animals that live in harsh environments are more vulnerable to other problems, such as disease. With pH below 5, adult fish die; at less than 4.5, lakes are entirely devoid of fish. Organic material lies undecayed on the bottom, and the sides of the lakes are covered with moss.

Although most acid enters lakes and ponds continuously, melting snow or heavy downpours can bring in excess runoff and temporarily raise the acid content of streams and lakes sharply. Temporary acidification can completely upset an ecosystem and result in massive fish kills.

Some organisms tolerate or even thrive in an acidic environment; these include some plants and mosses and black fly larvae. Frogs can tolerate lower acidity than fish, but they cannot live in a lake without food. Birds and mammals that depend on the lake for fish or plants also experience a decline in population. Therefore, whole freshwater ecosystems can be turned around, with organisms living in lakes that are not supposed to be there and other organisms absent that should be present.

THE EFFECTS OF ACID RAIN ON FORESTS AND AGRICULTURE

Sulfuric and nitric acids are detrimental to all plant life. Even if the soil is well-buffered, forests can be damaged by acid fog. Acid deposition of all sorts ruins the waxy coatings of leaves, harming the tree's ability to exchange water and gases with the atmosphere. Trees weakened by acid experience slower growth or injury and are more vulnerable to stresses such as pests or drought. Acid-damaged plants are easily identified: the leaves of leafy plants turn yellow, and damaged pine needles become reddish-orange at the tips before they die.

Acid rain also leaches soil nutrients, which stunts tree growth. When trees are deficient in calcium, they are less able to withstand freezing. "As with immune-compromised humans, plants may appear and function as if they were healthy, until exposed to even a routine stress or disease, then experience declines far more exaggerated than expected," said Professor Donald DeHayes of the University of Vermont in *Medical News Today* in 2005. DeHayes' study documented the depletion of calcium by acid rain that weakened high-altitude red spruce (*Picea rubens*) trees, making them more vulnerable to winter freezing. Other trees, such as the balsam fir (*Abies balsamea*), white pine (*Pinus strobes*), sugar maple (*Acer saccharum*), flowering dogwood (*Cornus florida*), and eastern hemlock (*Tsuga canadensis*) are also damaged in this way. Acid leaching also deposits metals in the topsoil. These metals—such as aluminum, lead, zinc, copper, and chromium—are toxic for trees, mosses, algae, some bacteria, and fungi.

Acid rain can destroy forest ecosystems. Acidic soil wipes out snail populations, which lowers the calcium intake of songbirds and causes them to produce eggs with thin shells. Birds and mammals that eat calcium-deficient plants may produce young that have weak or stunted bones; mammals may produce less milk.

The forests of the Appalachian Mountains from Maine to Georgia have been vulnerable to acid damage, in part because the soils there are not buffered. Researchers at the Cornell Lab of Ornithology in Ithaca, New York, in a 2002 article in *Birdscope* pinpointed the decline of a North American songbird, the wood thrush (*Hylocichla mustelina*), to acid rain. Calcium loss decreased the birds' breeding success, resulting in a population decline of 1.7% per year between 1966 and 1999. Many other bird species in the area are showing similar population declines. The Cornell study was the first to present large-scale evidence linking the decline of a North American bird to acid rain, although these links have been commonly found in Europe. If acid precipitation causes large swaths of trees to die, the life they support may mostly perish.

Germany's forests are in such a bad state that the term *Waldsterben*— or forest death—is well known in the country. A 1995 survey showed that more than half the trees in the nation's western forests, including the famed Black Forest, were in decline due to acid precipitation, magnesium deficiency, and the effects of other air pollutants. In 2004, nearly three-quarters of the trees were suffering decline from a combination of factors, including acid precipitation, drought, high ozone levels, and high levels of chemicals in the soil. According to a 2004 article in the *Guardian*, a British newspaper, the decline has been so rapid that Michael Hopf, a spokesman for Greenpeace Germany, said "We have pictures of the same forests taken in 2002 and 2004. You can see the damage very clearly." Germany's agriculture minister, Renate Künast, added, "The state of our forests is alarming. We must seize every possibility to reduce the burden on the forest ecosystem." Forests are suffering in other regions of the world, including Scandinavia, India, Russia, China, and Canada. High acidity can alter forest ecosystems as well as damage trees.

Acid precipitation may also damage crops, since the acid damages leaves and soil. In the developed nations, acid rain damage to agriculture is nullified by fertilizers that replace leached nutrients and lime that neutralizes the acid. However, in countries where farmers cannot afford these remedies, acid precipitation and increased soil acidity have an amplified effect. The World Bank has estimated China's overall annual forest and crop losses due to acid rain at $5 billion.

ACID DESTRUCTION OF CULTURAL MATERIALS

Acid rain takes a toll on stone buildings and other structures including those that are culturally significant. Just as limestone and marble buffer acidic water, acid rain dissolves buildings and statues made of these materials. The decreased pH of rain and fog is taking its toll on cultural objects, a phenomenon that has long been recognized. In the same year that he coined the term *acid rain* (1856), Robert Angus Smith wrote, "It has often been observed that the stones and bricks of buildings, especially under projecting parts, crumble more readily in large towns where coal is burnt . . . I was led to attribute this effect to the slow but constant action of acid rain."

Much of the world's architectural heritage is under siege from acid rain. Affected buildings include Westminster Abbey and St. Paul's Cathedral in London; the Taj Mahal in India; the Coliseum in Rome; the Acropolis in Greece; Egypt's temples at Karnak; and monuments in Krakow, Poland. In Sweden, medieval stained glass windows are thought to have been damaged by acid rain. In the United States, limestone buildings, such as the U.S. Capitol, show some acid rain damage.

The effects of acid rain on a stone building and statue. *(Adam Hart-Davis / Photo Researchers)*

In most cases, acid rain does not act alone to diminish the beauty of these buildings.

In limestone buildings, the calcite mineral that makes up the stone reacts with sulfur dioxide pollutants and moisture in the air to form the mineral gypsum. This mineral grows into a network of thin crystals that traps particles of dirt. A dark crust forms on its surface, turning the building black. Since the gypsum crust dissolves in water, it accumulates in sheltered areas protected from rainfall. The result is that much of the detail carved into many old limestone buildings appears black and dirty.

REDUCING ACID RAIN DAMAGE

The best way to reduce damage from acid rain is to lessen the emissions of SO_2 and NO_x into the atmosphere so that acid precipitation does not form. Methods for reducing acid-producing emissions also reduce other air pollutants. The alternative (and far less effective) approach is to mitigate the damage from acid precipitation. Just as rocks containing calcium carbonate buffer acidic water in nature, lime can be added to acidic lakes or ponds. The downside to this is that the lime only neutralizes the water and does nothing to change soil chemistry or improve forest health. This approach is expensive and must be done repeatedly if acid rain continues to fall. Despite these drawbacks, in countries such as Sweden and Norway, where they have little control over the pH of their rainfall, lakes and ponds are treated in this way in the hope that native fish populations will survive until the situation improves. In the eastern United States, adding lime to the soil has improved the health and productivity of maple trees used by the maple syrup industry. In this case, the expense is worth the economic advantage produced by this method.

WRAP-UP

Acid rain is an environmental problem that can be solved by keeping the acid-forming gases from entering the air. But although the solution may seem simple, it is not easy to implement. Industry must be motivated, especially economically, to design and use pollution-reducing technologies. Nonetheless, there has been some success in reducing acid rain-generating emissions by providing market-based economic incentives, which are described in Chapter 11. In most countries of Western Europe, acid rain-producing emissions have been greatly reduced. If acid rain is allowed to fall, damage can be ameliorated with neutralizing materials. This is a poorer solution to the problem because it is expensive and has only limited effectiveness.

Air Pollution Control

The air that Americans breathe is much cleaner than it once was—at least of some pollutants. This progress is the result of the Clean Air Act of 1970 and its later amendments, which set up targets for reductions in emissions of the major pollutants and programs for achieving them. The first step to controlling air pollution problems is to identify their source. Long-term monitoring of major and minor pollutants is set up in all regions of the United States and in other developed countries. Once problems are identified, pollutant emissions are reduced through the use of cleaner fuels and the installation of pollution-reducing technologies. Due to the development of new technologies, some of which are discussed in this chapter, the next decade or two should see reductions in emissions from power plants, industries, and motor vehicles, at least in the developed nations. Innovative market-based programs laid out in the 1990 amendment of the Clean Air Act have brought success in reducing some of the pollutants that cause acid rain.

AIR POLLUTION TRENDS

For the most part, the air over the United States has gotten cleaner since the Clean Air Act was passed in 1970. Figures published by the Environmental Protection Agency (EPA), show that between 1970 and 2003 the population of the United States grew by 39%, the gross domestic product (GDP) increased by 176%, vehicle miles traveled increased by 155%, and energy consumption increased by 45%. Yet, during this period, emissions of the six major pollutants (carbon monoxide, lead, nitrous oxides, ozone, sulfur dioxide, and particulates) dropped by 51%, and the total emission of toxic chemicals declined as well. The best success has been with lead; its gradual elimination from gasoline resulted in its near absence from emissions. For the acid rain producing compounds, sulfur dioxide (SO_2) fell 54% between 1983 and 2002, including a decrease of 39% over the more recent 10-year period of 1993 to 2002. Nitrous oxides (NO_x) increased by almost 17% from 1982 to 2001, but decreased 3% between 1992 and 2001. Improvements in SO_2 and NO_x emissions are attributed primarily to controls implemented under the EPA's Acid Rain Program, which began in 1995.

Many regions of the United States, including most urban and industrial regions, have seen great improvements in air quality. Despite this incredible progress, the air over much of the country is not yet clean. Many regions do not meet the standards of the Clean Air Act Amendment of 1990; there are too many cars, too much construction, and too much industry. Pollutants, both visible and invisible, continue to cause health risks to people and the environment.

California has led the way in air pollution control and the federal government has followed. California state bureaucracies lowered auto emissions standards in 1975, which meant that California cars needed catalytic converters two years before they were required in the rest of the country. The state eliminated lead from gasoline before it was required by the federal government, and put scrubbers and other pollution control devices on oil refineries and power and industrial plants. The South Coast Air Quality Management District monitors and regulates emissions from every other possible source, including dry cleaners, barbeque lighter fluid, and oil-based paints.

The Los Angeles Basin: *A Partial Success Story*

Between 1980 and 2005, Southern California's population grew by 60% and the number of cars doubled, according to an August 3, 2005, article in the *New York Times*. In that time, nitrogen oxides decreased by about two-thirds and carbon monoxide fell to about 20%. Data provided by the South Coast Air Quality Management District shows that the number of days the 8-hour ozone average exceeded federal standards dropped from 186 to 84. Extreme ozone events decreased too; in 1978, Southern California experienced 116 Stage I smog alerts and 23 Stage II smog alerts. In 2005, there were no ozone alerts at all. In fact, between 1999 and 2005 there was only one Stage I alert (in 2003); the last Stage II alert was in 1988.

Even though incredible progress has been made, residents of the Los Angeles Basin breathe dirty air on approximately one-third of the days each year. The relatively low levels of ozone are high enough to have health effects, particularly in children. A 10-year study released in 2004 of active children growing up in the Los Angeles basin revealed that those living in the worst areas for ozone had lung capacity of 10% to 20% less than those in areas with lower ozone levels. The study was headed by Dr. John Peters of the Keck School of Medicine of the University of Southern California in Los Angeles. In that

New York Times article of August 3, 2005, Peters said, "The statistics would show that you're going to die younger and be more likely to have more heart and lung disease."

The air in the Los Angeles Basin is getting worse again, at least in some areas. A growing source of pollution is the Port of Los Angeles, which receives 40% of the goods that come into the United States by ship. To pick up these goods, an average of 35,000 trucks visits the port each day. The ships, trucks, and heavy machinery at the port all run on highly polluting diesel fuel. Federal regulations put into place so far control only new, less-polluting engines. The older trucks, ships, and heavy machinery, which operate under the old standards, will continue to emit excess pollutants for many more years. The largest source of diesel particulates is ships, but they are difficult to regulate since they are governed by international law. Local attempts are being made at cleaning up these pollution sources, and any cleanup will happen none too soon. In Long Beach, a city located northeast of the ports, the cancer risk is twice that of west-central Los Angeles, and four times that in the mountains above the breezy Pacific Ocean. Particulates from diesel fuel account for 70% of the cancer risk.

Global trends in air pollution are mixed. In Europe, emissions of most pollutants are down and continuing to decline. In Asia, emissions are up tremendously; for example, emissions of NO_x approximately tripled between 1975 and 1997. The steep rise will continue as Asian countries work to improve their standard of living and, in doing so, burn more fossil fuels. Biomass burning, particularly of tropical rainforests, is increasing rapidly as well.

MONITORING AIR QUALITY

The Clean Air Act gives the EPA the job of establishing air quality standards and protecting public health and the environment. Primary air quality standards are set to protect human health; secondary standards protect human welfare as determined by other measures such as visibility, impact on crops, and damage to buildings. Regions that do not meet these standards must adopt air pollution reduction measures and lay out a timeframe for attainment. States that do not meet the standards must face sanctions, including the possible loss of highway funds.

To determine if air quality is improving or deteriorating, the EPA monitors air pollution around the country. The agency uses two methods for tracking air pollution: measurements and approximations. Measurements are made at more than 4,000 stations operated by state environmental agencies around the country. Of the six principal pollutants, only CO, SO_2, and particulates can be measured directly. Three other compounds are measured because they are precursors to the other pollutants: Ammonia is tracked because it reacts with nitric and sulfuric acids to form fine particulates, and nitrogen oxides and VOCs are monitored because they are precursors to ozone. Toxic air pollutants are also measured even though it is not mandated by the Clean Air Act. Data are added to the EPA's database hourly or daily, and yearly summaries are made for each station. By collecting and analyzing these data, the EPA can report on changes in emissions over time.

Increasingly, satellites are being used to monitor air pollution. Satellites detect and track pollutants as they move horizontally and vertically, which ground-based monitoring stations cannot do. Satellites provide a geographically continuous look at pollutants, rather than a station-only look. Additionally, they can be used to assess the impact of major events such as fires and dust movement from distant areas.

Emissions also are approximated based on estimates of vehicle miles traveled, fuel consumption, amounts of goods produced, and amounts of materials consumed. These estimates take into account the pollution control devices that are in place. Using all types of data, the EPA identifies regions that are not in compliance and works with them to improve their air quality. The Air Quality Index, shown on page 128, outlines the EPA's system for letting people know the quality of their air on a given day.

REDUCING EMISSIONS BY CHANGING ENERGY SOURCES

It is crucial that political leaders worldwide and the leaders of industries that cause air pollutant emissions take actions to reduce these emissions. The preferred approach for reducing air pollution is to keep the pollutants from entering the atmosphere. One way to do this is to reduce reliance on the energy sources that produce the most pollutants—fossil fuels—while phasing in alternative energy sources, such as hydropower, wind energy, geothermal energy, nuclear power, and solar energy (although a few of these have other environmental or health impacts that bear serious consideration). A change of this magnitude is difficult to accomplish. For one thing, large scale use of these energy sources would require large technological developments. For another, a change like this would require a transformation in the energy infrastructure. People would likely get energy from different sources depending on their location. To take advantage of its seemingly nonstop sunshine, Phoenix, Arizona, would be a suitable candidate for conversion to solar energy. Topeka, Kansas, on the Great Plains, could convert to windmills. A strategy like this would make energy production less centralized, not only regionally, but also down to the level of the individual household or consumer. A house might rely primarily on its own solar panel for energy, only using energy from a central source during times of peak need. But reducing reliance on fossil fuels to that extent will take time and motivation to develop the technologies and infrastructure. At this point, neither the people nor their governments are calling for major changes in energy sources, although a groundswell is beginning.

Since most energy for the foreseeable future will come from fossil fuels, another possibility for reducing emissions is burning cleaner fuels. Power plants, for example, could be restricted to burning natural gas and low-sulfur coal. Motor vehicles could burn natural gas exclusively. But such efforts would eliminate many fuels from poten-

Air Quality Index

The Air Quality Index (AQI) measures concentrations of CO, SO_2, NO_2, particulates, and ground-level ozone. The index is normalized so that, for each pollutant, values below 100 are healthful and those above 100 are not. For any day, the announced AQI is based on the pollutant that most exceeds standards; usually that pollutant is ozone. To make the AQI as easy to understand as possible, the EPA has divided the scale into six general categories:

- Good (0–50): Air quality is satisfactory; air pollution poses little or no risk.
- Moderate (51–100): Air quality is acceptable; there may be a moderate health concern for a very small number of individuals.

- Unhealthy for Sensitive Groups (101–150): People who are particularly sensitive to the harmful effects of certain air pollutants may be affected, although the general public will not.
- Unhealthy (151–200): Everyone may begin to experience health effects. Members of sensitive groups may experience more serious health effects.
- Very Unhealthy (201–300): Air quality in this range triggers a health alert; everyone may experience more serious health problems.
- Hazardous (over 300): Air quality in this range triggers health warnings of emergency conditions; the entire population may be affected.

tial use, and there are not enough supplies of these cleaner fuels to last very long.

REDUCING EMISSIONS FROM POWER PLANTS

The most practical way to reduce air pollution, and the one that has been favored so far, is the development of technologies that strip pollutants from emissions. Pollutants can be removed from all sources, including energy-producing plants and motor vehicles. Pollutants can be destroyed by thermal or catalytic combustion, they can be changed to a less toxic form, or they can be collected before they can enter the atmosphere.

There are several ways to remove pollutants from power plant emissions. **Scrubbers** eliminate particulates, SO_2, hydrogen sulfide, and other pollutants from waste gases as they pass through a solution before leaving the smokestack of coal-firing and other plants. **Baghouses**, enclosed structures that run emissions through filter bags in the same way as a vacuum cleaner, collect more than 98% of dry particulates. **Cyclones** collect toxic gases and particulates by using **centrifugal forces**, which are motions that proceed outward from a center. **Electronic precipitators** use static electricity to collect and remove unwanted substances that are suspended in very hot gases.

Technologies are being developed that will reduce power-plant emissions even more. One exciting new technology is that of **gasification**, which has been tested but has not yet been used in a full-scale power plant. Gasification produces **clean coal**, which is more efficient and produces far fewer emissions than normal coal. In gasification, coal is heated to about 2,500°F (1400°C) under pressure to produce syngas, a flammable gas that burns clean and is easily filtered for pollutants. Overall, clean-coal plants have emissions of NO_x, SO_2, mercury, and particulates that are about 80% less than traditional coal plants. Greenhouse-gas emissions, particularly CO_2, are also lower. Besides being low on emissions, syngas is extremely energy-rich and efficient. After being cleaned, syngas is combusted in a turbine that drives a generator; the waste heat powers a second, steam-powered generator. Gasification has other positive features: It makes dirty coal usable, which benefits regions where only dirty coal is available. Also, because the gas is cleansed before it is burned, gasification plants do not need expensive scrubbers.

Of course, gasification has a downside. Gasification plants costs 15% to 50% more to build and 20% to 30% more to run than normal coal-fired plants. Due to these additional costs, conversions will not become widespread without industry incentives. While a few plants use the technology in a small way, no large-scale plants will be running for many years. Some environmentalists are cautious about clean coal for other reasons: Coal mining itself damages the landscape and ecosystems, and developing clean coal may take emphasis away from developing more environmentally friendly alternatives, such as solar and wind power.

REDUCING EMISSIONS FROM MOTOR VEHICLES

Cars and other motor vehicles emit far less pollution than they did just a few decades ago. This is due to the higher emissions standards, improvements in fuel quality, and the installation of pollution-reducing technologies in many vehicles. One emission-reduction technology found in all modern cars in the United States is the **catalytic converter,** which is used to reduce and oxidize three pollutants: CO, NO_x, and VOCs. Catalytic converters are ceramic structures that are coated with metal catalysts. A **catalyst** is a substance that increases the rate of a chemical reaction without being consumed in the reaction. As car exhaust moves through the catalytic converter, the reduction catalyst, composed of platinum and rhodium, pulls a nitrogen atom from passing NO_x molecules and lets oxygen continue on as O_2. The nitrogen remains stuck to the catalyst until it bonds with another nitrogen atom to form N_2. Next, the oxidation catalyst, composed of platinum and palladium, oxidizes (burns) unburned VOCs and CO, so that they form CO_2. Finally, a sensor close to the engine alters the inflow of oxygen into the converter so that the oxygen level is high enough to allow oxidation but not so high that fuel efficiency is compromised. Catalytic converters are very effective, but they only work when hot; a lot of exhaust escapes when the car is warming up. One advantage to hybrid cars, discussed below, is that they use their battery packs to preheat the catalytic converter as soon as the engine is started.

An emerging option for reducing pollution from motor vehicles is **hybrid vehicles**. Hybrids use old technologies—a small internal combustion engine, an electric motor, and a rechargeable battery—and combine them in new ways to use fuel more efficiently. A normal car burns gasoline in its internal combustion engine for energy. When the brakes are applied, the vehicle's **kinetic energy**, the energy it holds because it is in motion, is lost. This wastes fuel and produces harmful tailpipe emissions. Hybrids also burn gasoline to run the combustion engine, but during braking they harvest the vehicle's kinetic energy to regenerate the battery, saving fuel and emissions. When the car accelerates or travels uphill, the battery boosts the engine's power so that the car uses less gas. Since hybrid engines are small, the car is lighter and takes less fuel to operate. When conditions are right for the car to run only on the electric motor and battery, such as at constant speeds around town, the gasoline engine shuts off completely.

Hybrids waste much less fuel than conventional vehicles, so they get up to 60 miles (100 km) per gallon. Because they make limited use of their combustion engine, hybrids reduce smog 90% or more, and greenhouse gas emissions by more than half. Hybrids are more expensive than standard cars of similar size and features, but they are much less expensive to operate. The initial release of hybrids has been phenomenally well received, and many more passenger vehicles will have hybrid counterparts in the coming years. One unfortunate turn of events is that in some vehicles, the hybrid technology is being used to help the car accelerate faster rather than to increase energy efficiency.

Fuel cell technology may someday be used in motor vehicles, but it is far from ready for that purpose right now. Like batteries, fuel cells convert chemical energy into electrical energy, but fuel cells do it very efficiently. Most of them harness the energy that is released when hydrogen and oxygen are converted into water. The by-products of this reaction are water vapor and heat. Unlike batteries, which are sealed so they contain all their chemicals, fuel cells have chemicals constantly flowing into them, so they never go dead. To convert a significant amount of energy, fuel cells must be stacked together. Many people see a great deal of promise in fuel cell technology. Besides the incredible efficiency when pure hydrogen is used, the oxygen needed for hydrogen-oxygen fuel cells exists in the air and so is widely available. In addition, vehicles run with hydrogen fuel cells have no emissions—no pollution at all.

Fuel-cell use is in its infancy, but it is entering a rapid growth phase. Fuel cells are replacing batteries in portable electronic devices, where they are advantageous since they last longer and are rechargeable. Demand for alternative energy sources after recent

Energy and Energy Efficiency

The First Law of Thermodynamics can be summarized this way: Energy can neither be created nor destroyed. Energy can be transferred from one body to another, or it can change form; it cannot just appear or disappear. Chemical energy can become heat energy or kinetic energy can become mechanical energy or any other combination. For example, the energy in gasoline is solar energy that was stored in plants. Burned in a car, that energy becomes mechanical work, which moves the car. In this way, combustion engines, gas turbines, and batteries can be thought of as energy conversion devices.

Energy transfer is rarely 100% efficient. A normal car turns only about 20% of the energy content of the gasoline it burns into mechanical work; the rest becomes waste heat. Hydrogen and oxygen fuel cells are more efficient than other energy conversion methods—between 65% and 80%—but if a hydrocarbon or alcohol fuel is the source of hydrogen, the efficiency is reduced to 30% to 40%. When this hydrogen fuel is put into a motor, the efficiency of the fuel cell drops to between 24% and 32%. Battery-powered cars are much more efficient, about 72%, but that ignores how the electricity to power the car was generated. If the electricity comes from a combustion power plant, whether nuclear, hydroelectric, or solar, the efficiency is reduced to about 26%. If the electricity comes from hydroelectric power, which harnesses the kinetic energy released by falling water, the efficiency is about 65%.

energy price spikes is making the development and spread of fuel-cell technology even more attractive.

Unfortunately, there are many problems with fuel-cell technology. Most importantly, hydrogen is not an energy source; it is an energy carrier, and so fuel cells are only energy conversion devices. Hydrogen is difficult to store and use. One solution is to use a reformer, which turns hydrocarbon or alcohol fuels, such as natural gas, propane, or methanol, into hydrogen. Unfortunately, this process requires electricity and so greatly decreases fuel-cell efficiency and increases the production of waste heat and gases. In his 2003 book, *The Hype about Hydrogen: Fact and Fiction in the Race to Save the Climate*, Dr. Joseph Romm points out that hydrogen from natural gas, which is the only practical hydrogen source at this time, produces greenhouse gases. Romm also mentions other technical and safety issues that suggest that a large-scale conversion to hydrogen is a long way into the future.

In a June 24, 2005, *Science* article, a team of Stanford University researchers suggested that the drawbacks of using hydrogen fuel cells would be minimized and the pollutants would remain negligible if the hydrogen was pumped into fuel cells using wind power. "Switching from a fossil-fuel economy to a hydrogen economy would be subject to technological hurdles, the difficulty of creating a new energy infrastructure, and considerable conversion costs but could provide health, environmental, climate and economic benefits and reduce the reliance on diminishing oil supplies." The costs may be worth the inevitable problems that would need to be faced.

THE POLITICS OF EMISSION REDUCTIONS

The previous sections describe technological methods, both current and in development, for reducing pollutant emissions. But adding scrubbers to power plants or catalytic converters to cars costs money, so people and businesses must be required or at least encouraged to take these emission-reducing steps. For more than three decades, the Clean Air Act has been the motivator and guide for emissions reductions in the United States. By the provisions of the Clean Air Act, individual plants are responsible for meeting pollution guidelines by monitoring and restricting their own emissions. The goal is an overall reduction in emissions over time.

The 1990 Amendment to the Clean Air Act outlined a unique, market-based method for reducing the emissions of some pollutants, primarily SO_2. Called "cap-and-trade," this method requires the EPA to set a countrywide "cap" for annual SO_2 emissions. Program participants receive allowances for the amount of SO_2 they are permitted to discharge each year. The allowances can be used, traded to another participant, or banked for future use. Because allowances can be traded for cash, companies have a monetary incentive for developing emission-saving technologies. If a plant exceeds its total allowances—those that it has been assigned this year and those it has banked for future use—it is fined. To be sure emissions lessen over time, the cap set by the EPA will be decreased each year until the permanent cap is reached in 2010. At that time, annual SO_2 emissions will be approximately 50% below 1980 levels. The success of cap-and-trade for SO_2 has resulted in a program being set up to regulate NO_x. This was not done initially because NO_x has a much larger variety of sources and so is harder to control. Nonetheless, a limited program has been initiated to regulate NO_x emissions from power plants and from motor vehicles in some Eastern and Midwestern states.

"The annual allowance auction is a part of the reason that the Acid Rain Program's cap-and-trade approach shows such remarkable results," said former EPA Administrator Christie Whitman in a press release on March 26, 2003. "The cap-and-trade mechanism under the Acid Rain Program has reduced emissions and improved human and environmental health earlier, and at less cost, than would have occurred with more conventional approaches."

Environmentalists and capitalists have strongly supported cap-and-trade programs for the reduction of acid rain-causing pollutants. These programs have been very successful. With a compliance level of over 99%, pollutant emissions have been greatly reduced. By 2005, SO_2 emissions were 41% lower than in 1980, and NO_x emissions were less than half what they would likely have been without the program. This has resulted in a decrease in acid deposition in the eastern United States of as much as 36% relative to 1980 in acid-prone regions. In some areas, the number of acidic lakes and streams has decreased by one-fourth to one-third, although in some areas there has been no change. The number of acidic lakes in the Adirondacks has decreased from 13% to 8% since the early 1990s.

Cap-and-trade systems have been proposed for wider adoption but are difficult to implement since tracking the number of pollutants and their behavior after they are emitted is complex. Capitalists favor these programs for most other pollutants, but environmentalists and some policymakers do not concur. Mercury has been the topic of recent disagreements. A cap-and-trade program for mercury would allow a polluter or polluters in a single geographical area to buy or trade for pollution credits, potentially resulting in high concentrations of the metal. Because airborne mercury travels far from its source, atmospheric processes may concentrate the fallout. Either of these scenarios could create mercury "hot spots" in which concentrations of the metal rise far higher than is safe. Because mercury is extremely toxic, especially to children and fetuses, locally high levels of mercury compounds could cause acute damage to nearby residents. Cap-and-trade programs work for other pollutants because the effects of locally high concentration of those compounds are not so dire.

POSITIVE STEPS YOU CAN MAKE

Pollutants are the by-product of the lifestyle people in the developed world take for granted. Pollutants are generated when we power up our computers, cook our meals, or drive to a baseball game; they are also generated by the manufacture of products such as computers and cars. Reducing the pollutants we manufacture is as easy as reducing the amount of energy we use and the number of products we consume. While these strategies require some thought and perhaps sacrifice, they can yield important returns.

The major sources of air pollution created by people in the developed world involve transportation. For ideas on how to reduce pollution from transportation sources and how to reduce pollution at home, see the tables on pages 136 and 137.

Decreasing biomass burning can also help lower pollutant emissions and allow forest plants to absorb greenhouse gases. Although it may seem impossible to have an effect on forests that are half a world away, consumers do have power. To help reduce biomass burning:

⊕ Buy only those wood products that are certified by the Canadian Standards Association, the Forestry Stewardship Council, and the Sustainable Forestry Initiative and other certification programs for sustainable forestry.
⊕ Beware of beef from fast-food outlets, which are often supplied by cattle raised in cleared rain forest lands.
⊕ Support organizations that work toward forest preservation in the tropics and at home.

Reducing Air Pollution from Transportation Sources

WHAT TO DO	HOW
Use less gasoline	Use public transportation, walk, ride a bike, carpool
Buy a "green" vehicle	Choose a vehicle that the EPA green vehicles Web site states emits less pollution and greenhouse gases
Look into new technologies	Check out hybrid cars or cars powered by liquid natural gas or fuel cells to see if they are cost effective
Be frugal when driving	Avoid drive-through lines, keep car serviced and tires inflated, stay within the speed limit, do not accelerate quickly
Be careful when filling the gas tank	Fill during the cooler evening hours to avoid evaporation; don't spill or overfill when filling the gas tank

Reducing Air Pollution at Home

WHAT TO DO	HOW
Use energy-efficient appliances	Purchase energy-efficient appliances and lighting, and be sure they are operating well; be sure woodstoves and fireplaces are well maintained
Save electricity	Turn off the lights, television, and computer, especially overnight; keep the thermostat set to reasonable temperatures
Use vegetation	Planting deciduous trees around the house will provide shade in the summer and let in warmth and light during the winter
Consume sensibly	Buy only products that are really needed; buy products that are made to save energy
Reduce, reuse, and recycle	Recycled materials use less energy than it takes to make a new product from new materials. Choose recycled products and those that have less packaging

WRAP-UP

The best hope for large-scale pollution reduction is for the development of new technologies, the expanded use of old ones, and increased economic incentives to do both these things. In the long term, air pollution problems need to be solved by substituting alternative energy sources for fossil fuels, and the political and social support for the enormous amount of research and development needed is just beginning. Smaller steps to reducing air pollution include the development and widespread adoption of pollutant-reducing technologies. People can make a difference by consuming sensibly and avoiding burning fossil fuels. The United States may be moving toward a system similar to some European countries in which the cost of electricity and gasoline is heavily taxed to better reflect its environmental costs and to encourage the development of new technologies.

The Atmosphere Above Cities

C ities influence their own weather and climate, including air temperature, humidity, wind speed and direction, and amount of precipitation. These differences are due largely to the altering of natural terrain—tall buildings and pavement have very different effects on their surroundings than vegetated areas and waterways have on theirs. The emission of heat by vehicles, power plants, and factories also alters temperature. The increased temperature found in cities is known as the **urban heat island effect**.

THE DIFFERENCES BETWEEN URBAN AND RURAL WEATHER AND CLIMATE

Temperature is the largest climatic difference between the country and the city. In winter and summer, at night and in the daytime, cities are warmer than rural areas. On a hot summer day, the temperature difference can be as great as 10°F (6°C). The intensity of the temperature

An Extreme Urban Heat Island: Phoenix, Arizona

Climatologists say that Phoenix, Arizona, and its environs—also known as the Valley of the Sun—is the world's foremost urban heat island. Phoenix lies at 33°N in the Sonora Desert, where descending hot, dry air brings more evaporation than precipitation. The Valley of the Sun boasts 325 days of sunshine and less than 8 inches (20 km) of rain per year. Housing prices are low compared with nearby California.

With a population approaching 4 million, these attractions have made the Valley one of the top three fastest growing metropolitan areas in the United States.

The Sonora Desert, the landscape surrounding Phoenix, consists of cactus, trees, and scrub. The terrain is varied, with rocky soil and craggy mountains. The influx of people into the Valley of the Sun

(continues)

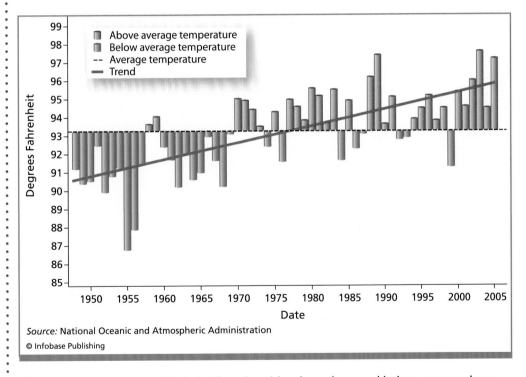

Source: National Oceanic and Atmospheric Administration

© Infobase Publishing

The average temperature in July in Phoenix, with values above and below average shown. The increase in average annual temperature from 1948 to 2005 is 0.91°F (0.50°C) per decade. *(Data provided by NOAA's National Climatic Data Center)*

(continues)

has brought a steady march of red tile roofs, strip malls, and parking lots, which has drastically altered the temperature. In 1948, the mean temperature for July was 91.2°F (32.9°C), but by 2005 it had risen to 97.2°F (36.2°C), an increase of 0.91°F (0.50°C) per decade. In that same time, the nighttime low temperature rose more than 10°F (6.5°C).

Climatologists at the Decision Center for a Desert City at Arizona State University have developed a meteorological modeling tool to project future urban heat island effects. The researchers discovered that a 1% increase in nighttime temperatures results in a 2% rise in water usage in single-family homes—a significant effect in a desert city. Future population growth will expand and intensify the urban heat island effect, according to their model.

Satellite images of the Phoenix area do not show a large swath of heat, but rather heat with pockets of coolness where there are more trees or where the land is less developed. Temperatures along one major road revealed a 10°F (6.5°C) nighttime temperature difference between the city and a neighboring rural area. Infrared photos of the city at night revealed a downtown park with 30°F (16.7 °C) lower temperature than the surrounding streets.

The way land is developed can make a difference. The Tucson metropolitan area, about 100 miles (160 km) southeast of Phoenix, has a population approaching one million and an elevation of approximately 1,000 feet (300 m) higher than Phoenix. In Tucson, houses are spread farther apart, and there is much more natural landscaping. The ground surface has less concrete and many more natural materials. Tucson's summertime highs are on average 4.5°F (2.5°C) cooler and lows are more than 10°F (5.5°C) cooler than in the Valley.

difference between urban and rural areas depends on the area's weather and climate, its proximity to water bodies, and its topography.

There are two main causes of urban heat island effect. One is the waste heat that is produced by the cars, buildings, and factories that are concentrated in cities. The second is the difference in ground cover. In rural areas, plants absorb sunlight, so only a small percentage reaches the ground; the rest remains as light. Water provides chances for evaporative cooling. In cities, the ground is covered with pavement, buildings, asphalt, and other man-made materials, which absorb sunlight and re-radiate it as heat. Much of the release of heat takes place at night, when air temperatures cool and the heat has somewhere to go. As a result, nighttime minimum temperatures are often much higher in cities than in nearby rural areas. Water runs off the pavement into sewers and very little of the precipitation evaporates, so there is much less evaporative cooling. An extreme case of urban heat island effect is found in Phoenix, Arizona (see sidebar on page 139).

Cities have wind speeds about 20% to 30% less than their rural neighbors due to the increased friction of air flowing over structures. Winds tend to flow into a city, because the warm air created within an urban area rises, sucking in air from the surrounding regions. Particulates in city air serve as nuclei for condensation of fog or rain, and precipitation over some large cities is 5% to 10% higher than over nearby rural areas.

THE EFFECTS OF AN URBAN HEAT ISLAND

Cities have high air pollution due to the high density of industry, motor vehicles, and solid-waste burning. Particulates scatter solar radiation, reduce the sunlight that reaches the city, and serve as nuclei for water droplets, which form haze and reduce visibility. Particulates also absorb some of the heat radiated from the Earth's surface, contributing to urban heat island effect. When there is a temperature inversion, pollutants become trapped in the air and concentrations can become extreme.

When urban heat island effect causes the air above a city to warm enough, it rises, forming clouds and thunderstorms. Storms are more common over cities and precipitation is higher, particularly in humid regions. Atlanta, Georgia, is 5°F to 8°F (2.8°C to 4.4°C) hotter than outlying areas; the excess heat brings early morning rain showers to the city, something rarely seen in the surrounding areas.

Having somewhat balmier city temperatures may be a good thing, at least in the winter in cold-weather cities such as Boston, Cincinnati, and New York. Warmer air temperatures cut down the need for heating and result in lower fuel demands, which in turn result in reduced pollution. Unfortunately, the situation is reversed in the summer; additional heat increases demand for cooling and, therefore, demand for fuel. For every 1°F (0.6°C) increase in summertime temperature, there is a 1.5% to 2.0% increase in energy use. So, in cities with high urban heat island effect, between 3% and 8% of the fuel consumed is to compensate for the increased temperatures. This can result in significantly higher energy costs in warm weather cities such as Phoenix and Los Angeles. Of course, increased fuel use increases pollution, which increases temperatures over the city. In addition, higher temperatures accelerate the chemical reaction that produces ground-level ozone.

Curbing Urban Heat Island Effect: Sacramento, California

The mission of the Urban Heat Island Pilot Project (UHIPP), launched by the EPA in 1998, is to research and develop pilot projects that reduce urban heat island effect. Five cities were chosen based on the magnitude of their ozone problem, the potential benefits of the project to the city, the availability of data, and local interest in the project. One of the chosen cities—Sacramento, California, the state capital—is located on the eastern side of the Central Valley, close to the Sierra Nevada foothills. This sprawling city is home to approximately 400,000 people, with another 1.4 million spread over a total of 984 square miles (2,550 km²). Sacramento summers are sunny, hot, and dry. Average high temperature for July and August is 88°F (31°C), and the use of air conditioning is high. Winters are cool, and there are about 18 inches (46 cm) of rainfall a year. Like other sprawling, arid western cities, Sacramento has a big problem with ground level ozone, 70% of which comes from vehicles. Reducing NO_x emissions from vehicles is an important goal for the city.

Thermal sensing of Sacramento shows a dramatic difference between temperatures on various types of ground surfaces. The starkest contrast is between the cool, blue Sacramento River, which measures about 85°F to 96°F (29°C to 36°C), and the hot red rooftops, which are about 140°F (60°C). Models of the metropolitan area indicate that the afternoon temperature increase due to urban heat island effect is between 0.9°F and 1.8°F (0.5°C and 1°C). The models also show that an increase in vegetation in the city could reduce temperature by 2.9°F (1.6°C), which would also reduce ground-level ozone significantly. The U.S. Department of Energy has shown that a great deal of energy could be saved if Sacramento's urban heat island effect were reduced. For example, placing eight mature deciduous shade trees around each residence, eight around office buildings, and four around commercial buildings resulted in an overall reduction in carbon emissions of 92,000 tons and a potential savings of approximately $26 million.

As part of the UHIPP program, Sacramento is making on-the-ground changes. It has launched several demonstration projects, including installing reflective and green roofs, planting shade trees, and showcasing cool pavements. Sacramento Shade, the largest shade tree planting program in the United States, reports that as of September, 2006, 375,000 trees had been planted near homes, schools, and public buildings.

Sacramento's planned steps to decrease urban heat island effect include:

- ⊕ installing cool or vegetated green roofs to reflect the Sun's energy
- ⊕ planting trees and vegetation to prevent sunlight from striking windows and walls and to increase **evapotranspiration**, the loss of water by evaporation in plants
- ⊕ switching to cool paving materials, which have higher solar reflectance and minimize heat transfer to the surrounding air.

WRAP-UP

The strategies planned by Sacramento to decrease urban heat island effect would work in many communities. The first step to decreasing excess urban temperatures is to educate community leaders and residents about urban heat islands and to introduce strategies to reduce

A thermally sensed image of Sacramento, California. Hot areas are red, and cool areas are blue. Note the cool Sacramento River passing through the hot city. *(GHCC / National Space Science & Technology Center (NSSTC) / NASA)*

their effects. Ideally, steps to combat the effect should be designed and implemented by entire communities, but in the absence of large-scale efforts, individual residents can also make a difference simply by planting trees and decreasing the use of man-made materials around their properties. Reducing energy use reduces waste heat, another cause of urban heat island effect.

PART FOUR

HUMAN INFLUENCE ON THE ATMOSPHERE: GLOBAL IMPACTS

Ozone Loss in the Stratosphere

Ozone (O_3) is a pollutant and a greenhouse gas in the troposphere. In the stratosphere, O_3 protects the planet from the Sun's most damaging high-energy ultraviolet radiation, completely blocking out the lethal UVC and much of the dangerous UVB. Stratospheric ozone is found mostly in the ozone layer. Without the ozone layer, only the most primitive life forms could exist on our planet. Now the ozone layer is being destroyed by chlorofluorocarbons (CFCs) and other man-made chemicals, which break down the O_3. Fortunately, countries are phasing out the use of these chemicals according to the terms of the Montreal Protocol, a singularly successful global response to an environmental problem. After decades of declining stratospheric ozone levels, the rate of growth in the size of the **ozone hole**—the area around Antarctica and the southern continents that has had severely depleted springtime ozone levels—is declining, and the hole is likely to begin to decrease in size later this decade.

THE ASSAULT OF CHLOROFLUOROCARBONS ON OZONE

Under natural circumstances, the rate of ozone destruction in the ozone layer is nearly equal to the rate of ozone creation. In recent decades, this system has been knocked out of balance. The stratospheric ozone layer is under attack by man-made organic chemicals such as chlorofluorocarbons (CFCs), halons, methyl bromide, carbon tetrachloride, and methyl chloroform. CFCs are the most dangerous because they are the most abundant. For decades, they were widely used as refrigerants, cleaning agents, spray-can propellants, and building blocks for insulating foams because they are cheap, nontoxic, nonflammable, and chemically nonreactive.

The confidence of people in these chemicals took a hit in 1973 when a graduate student, Mario Molina, calculated the effects of CFCs on the ozone layer. When his academic advisor, Sherwood Rowland, looked at Molina's work, the two men checked and rechecked it for errors but could find none. After the review of some colleagues, they published their chilling findings: CFCs rise to the Earth's stratosphere and destroy its fragile ozone shield. Molina and Rowland won the 1995 Nobel Prize in chemistry for their momentous work.

Molina and Roland discovered that the properties that make CFCs useful also make them dangerous. Because they are nonreactive, these chemicals travel unaltered through the troposphere into the stratosphere. In the stratosphere, UV breaks them down into smaller components. One of these, chlorine (Cl), wrenches one of the O ions away from an O_3 molecule, quickly releases it, and then moves on to break apart another O_3. This process creates an O_2 molecule and an O molecule, neither of which protects the planet from UV radiation. The Cl from only one CFC molecule can destroy up to 100,000 ozone molecules before it itself is destroyed.

Initially, some scientists doubted Molina and Rowland's calculations, thinking that there must be a way for CFCs to break down in the troposphere. They thought this was likely because the measurements did not show the global decline in stratospheric ozone they expected; no one anticipated that the ozone decline would be found in a specific place during a particular season. Atmospheric scientists were stunned in 1985 when members of the British Antarctic Survey (BAS) published a paper in *Nature* showing that up to 50% of the stratospheric ozone layer had disappeared over Antarctica during the previous three springs. Members of BAS, including J.C. Farman, B.G. Gardiner, and J.D. Shanklin, had been monitoring ozone over the Antarctic since 1957 to study the role of O_3 in the stratosphere, and for 20 years they observed a regular seasonal cycle of ozone concentration. Then, in the early 1980s, they discovered that springtime ozone levels were decreasing dramatically over Antarctica.

THE ANTARCTIC OZONE HOLE

Atmospheric scientists wondered: Why was an ozone hole forming over Antarctica, and why in the spring? Years of work have found answers to these questions. Global atmospheric circulation patterns carry air and its pollutants toward the poles. During the long, dark Antarctic winter, a strong wind, called the polar vortex, circles the pole in the middle to lower stratosphere, trapping frigid air over the polar region. When air temperatures get cold enough, below approximately -110°F (-80°C), polar stratospheric clouds (PSCs) form. Rather than growing from pure water like other clouds, PSCs arise from droplets of nitric acid and water ice. These clouds are crucial to ozone destruction because the CFCs attach to the droplets' surfaces and then break apart, releasing molecular chlorine (Cl_2). In the spring, when the Sun's light first hits the PSCs, UV breaks the Cl_2 into chlorine ions (Cl) and ozone destruction begins. As spring progresses, the Antarctic air mass warms and begins to move northward over the southern continents—Australia, New Zealand, southern South America, and Africa. When the ozone hole shifts over them, UV levels rise more than 20%.

When it was discovered in 1981, the hole was only 900,000 square miles (2 million km^2). Since then, it has continued to grow in size, although its exact dimensions vary from year to year. In 2006, ozone levels were at a record low for the south polar area, and the hole was nearly as large as the hole of 11.4 million square miles (28 million

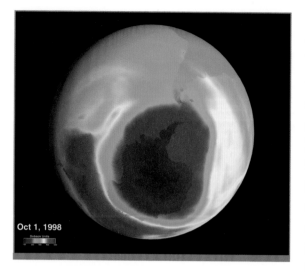

Oct 1, 1998

Dobson Units

Stratospheric ozone levels, with low values shown in magenta and purple. This figure shows the ozone hole sitting over Antarctica. *(NASA)*

km^2) that grew in 2000—more than three times the size of the United States. Although the trend is for larger holes, the size of each year's hole depends on stratospheric temperature, since PSCs are crucial to formation of the ozone hole. The duration of the ozone hole each spring has also increased. It is now present between August and early December and is at its peak in September and early October.

Ozone loss also occurs over the Arctic in the springtime, although the depletion is not great enough to be called a hole. The Arctic ground surface is more complex, with land, water, and ice; thus air circulates more and the temperatures do not get as cold. PSCs are less able to form here and so less chlorine separates from CFCs. However, Arctic winter temperatures are extremely variable, and in recent years the Arctic stratosphere has grown colder and more humid, which promotes PSC formation. Late in the spring, the ozone-depleted air moves south over the world's most populated regions—Europe, North America, and Asia. So, although there is much less ozone depletion in the north polar area, it can affect many more people. Since 1978, UVB levels have grown about 4% per decade at 40°N, the latitude of New York City.

Ozone loss has important consequences for human health. Ozone depletion is most pronounced at high latitudes and less prominent near the equator. However, the rate of non-melanoma skin cancer is strongly linked to accumulated dosage of UVB, which enters the atmosphere in greater amounts near the equator. Therefore, a small ozone loss at low latitudes provides a much larger risk to human health than a larger

UV and Skin Damage

UV radiation is made of three varieties of short wavelength, high-energy waves. The ozone layer blocks virtually all of the highest energy UVC waves. Some UVB gets through the ozone layer; in humans, it produces sunburn and around 90% of all skin cancers. UVA waves tan the skin and cause redness; large amounts can weaken the skin's immune system and can cause premature aging.

A suntan is the skin's way of protecting itself from solar radiation. Human skin is made of three cell layers. From the surface to the interior, they are the squamous, the basal, and the melanocytes. When bombarded by UV, the melanocytes produce the dark pigment melanin, which absorbs some of the incoming radiation and creates a suntan. Rather than being a sign of good health, however, a tan means that the skin has been injured.

Every day, new skin cells push older cells up to the skin surface, where they fall off. After excess UV exposure, this process directs damaged cells to die, which is why sunburned skin peels. In some damaged skin, the repair system malfunctions, and damaged cells continue to accumulate and grow. Skin cancer is the abnormal growth of skin cells in any of the three skin layers.

Skin cancer is nearly as common as all other cancers combined. More than one million new skin cancer cases are diagnosed in Americans each year, and almost half of all Americans will develop a cancerous skin lesion at least once by the age of 65. Basal cell and squamous cell cancers are usually superficial, slow growing, and treatable if they are found early. These non-melanoma cancers are correlated with lifetime UV exposure. **Melanoma**, which targets the deeper layers of the skin, is much less common but much more lethal: According to the Skin Cancer Foundation, 80% of the nearly 10,000 skin cancer deaths per year are due to melanoma. There is a correlation between serious sunburn in young children and the eventual appearance of melanoma, even decades later.

As more people move to the sunny southern and western United States, skin cancer rates are increasing. Non-melanoma cancers are growing at about 5% a year, while melanoma grows at about 3% a year. Since 1973, the melanoma mortality rate has risen by 50%. Although skin cancer was once a disease for middle-aged and older Americans, now one-quarter of the people who develop melanoma are under 40. Adequate skin protection requires sunscreen that blocks both UVA and UVB. The higher the Sun Protection Factor (SPF) of sunscreen, the more defense it offers. Hats, clothing, sunglasses, and shade are also important.

loss at higher latitudes. For example, a 10% ozone loss at the equator equals a 30% loss at 50°N in terms of its biological effect.

THE MONTREAL PROTOCOL

Molina and Rowland's results were serious enough to inspire representatives of several countries to take action to save the ozone layer. As early as 1978, the United States and most Scandinavian countries banned CFCs in spray cans. The identification of the Antarctic ozone hole made the threat seem more real, and for the first time, world political leaders mobilized around an environmental issue. The Montreal Protocol on Substances that Deplete the Ozone Layer, an agreement that controls the production and consumption of ozone-depleting substances, was ratified just two years after the discovery of the hole was made public. The protocol became effective in 1989. Since then, several amendments have been signed to increase the number of controlled substances and regulate the trade of substances between developing and developed nations, all with the goal of returning the ozone layer to its 1970s status.

The Montreal Protocol currently controls 96 substances. For most, usage is not frozen but is being phased out. Each cutback has two timescales: one for developed countries and another for developing ones. The phaseout schedule for the developing nations is looser, with a one-decade grace period for most substances so that economic development is not hindered. The speed of the reduction depends on the chemical's harmfulness. CFCs were phased out in the developed countries in 1995 and must be fully phased out in the developing nations by 2010. HCFCs, which are much less ozone-depleting than some chemicals, are on the following phaseout schedule for the developed nations: 35% in 2004, 65% in 2010, 90% in 2015, 99.5% in 2020, and 100% in 2030. The final 0.5% will be available only for essential purposes. Worldwide, HCFCs will be frozen at 2015 levels in 2016 and will be phased out by 2040. The Montreal Protocol requires industrialized nations to donate $510 million to develop technologies to aid in the move away from ozone-depleting chemicals. Compounds that are essential for the health and safety of society will continue to be produced if there is no known substitute, but this provision is reviewed annually.

The Montreal Protocol was the first international agreement designed to solve an important environmental problem. Some people fear that some of the momentum has been lost in the years since the original protocol was ratified by 188 countries, because the 2003 amendment was ratified by only 81 countries. Nonetheless, CFC consumption has been greatly reduced: Between 1986 and 2004, CFC use went from 1.1 million to approximately 70,000 ODP tons. (ODP tons are obtained by multiplying the natural tons by the ozone depleting potential [ODP] of a substance relative to freon-11.) Had use continued to climb at the pre-1980 rate, CFC consumption would have reached 3 million tons in 2010 and 8 million in 2060. By 2050, atmospheric CFC levels would have been 10 times higher than in 1980, with an additional 20 million skin cancer cases in the United States and 130 million globally.

Tropospheric CFC levels peaked in 2000 and are now decreasing by almost 1% a year. CFCs take 10 to 20 years to travel through the lower atmosphere into the stratosphere; therefore, stratospheric chlorine levels will continue to rise for 20 to 30 years. In addition, CFCs can survive in the stratosphere for many years. The presence of residual CFCs is one of the reasons that the ozone hole is still getting bigger. Other reasons for the continued growth of the ozone hole are that some substitutes for CFCs and other ozone-depleting chemicals also destroy ozone, but at a lower rate. There is also a thriving black market in CFCs as developing nations sell their stocks to developed nations. Some CFC substitutes contribute to other environmental damage; for example, HCFCs and HFCs are powerful greenhouse gases.

Scientists predict that the first healing of the Antarctic ozone hole will occur late in the 2000s, and the ozone layer will reach pre-1980 concentrations in 2068. Global ozone levels will not match pre-1950 levels for another 100 to 200 years. Nonetheless, it is estimated that the international ban on ozone-depleting chemicals will prevent 1.5 million skin cancer cases each year in the United States alone.

THE EFFECTS OF OZONE LOSS ON AGRICULTURE AND HUMAN HEALTH

Future decades of low stratospheric ozone could have a significant impact on agriculture and on human health. Two-thirds of the approximately 300 species of food plants that have been tested show some sensitivity to UVB, including a slowing of growth and development and a decrease in yields. The damage is done to the plant's genetic code, its DNA, which affects its form and function and may make it more vulnerable to insect infestations and disease.

Although skin cancer rates have increased alarmingly, it is difficult to separate the effects of ozone loss from those of increased Sun exposure due to people moving to lower latitudes. In the United States, it is estimated that a 1% loss of stratospheric ozone results in a rise of approximately 3% in non-melanoma skin cancers and 1% in fatal melanomas. Increased UV exposure is also increasing eye damage since the cornea absorbs UV light. High doses cause "snow-blindness," temporary corneal damage that disappears after several hours, but chronic exposure brings about cataracts. Increased UV may also cause immune system suppression and reduce peoples' defenses against infectious diseases and some cancers. Some of these effects are already being seen near the Antarctic ozone hole.

THE EFFECTS OF OZONE LOSS ON THE NATURAL ENVIRONMENT

People can stay out of the Sun and they may be able to plant their crops in different locations, but the plants and animals of the natural world are not so flexible. Ozone loss affects long-lived trees, predominantly conifers and evergreens, in which UVB damage accumulates. Some trees in temperate forests change form and slow their growth. In tundra and subarctic areas, which are most likely to experience increased UV, the plants become more vulnerable to other problems, such as insect infestation. In the forests of southern South America, UVB decreases the growth of herbaceous and grassy plants with no

Living Under the Ozone Hole

The effects of the ozone hole are best seen at the site of the world's southernmost city, Punta Arenas, Chile, at 53°S. Punta Arenas suffers from long, frigid winters with six hours of daylight and temperatures around 32°F (0°C). In the past, springtime was a time to celebrate. Yet for the past two decades, spring is when the ozone hole spreads over the city, turning the sky white and causing the Sun's reflection to become blinding. Officials have introduced a 4-level, color-coded "solar stoplight" as follows: green (normal), yellow (wear a hat and sunglasses), orange (apply sunscreen) and red (stay in the shade "as much as possible"). When the light is at yellow, the noontime Sun can burn skin in 21 minutes. When it is red, it takes just five.

In September 2000, for the first time, the ozone hole opened directly over the city; a 56% reduction in ozone was recorded. The hole currently opens over the city a few times a year, a problem that may persist until the middle of this century. In the past, sunburns and skin cancer were virtually nonexistent in Punta Arenas. Now three times as many residents have malignant melanoma as do people in other parts of the world. The situation may be worse in Santiago, Chile's capital, where ozone loss is less but the Sun's angle is higher. Between 1992 and 1998, the melanoma rates more than doubled in Santiago. These increases will likely grow since it takes 10 to 20 years for skin cancers to develop.

change in woody plants. In the plant species showing the greatest effect, DNA damage in leaf tissue is directly related to the amount of ground level UVB.

Ozone loss affects marine ecosystems as well as terrestrial ones. Photosynthesizing phytoplankton are the planet's single greatest source of O_2 and form the base of the marine food chain. These organisms may respond to increased UV by sinking deeper into the water, decreasing their contact with visible light and their ability to photosynthesize. During times of ozone depletion, Antarctic phytoplankton produce up to 12% less food energy, which equals a 2% to 4% annual loss. Lower food production at the base of the food chain means less energy for reproduction and less for other organisms to eat. A 16% depletion of ozone could result in a 5% loss of phytoplankton. Krill, a type of zooplankton, depend on phytoplankton for food and are the favorite food of baleen whales. If ozone destruction reduces the productivity of phytoplankton significantly, populations of several whale species could decline.

WRAP-UP

Damaging effects have been seen in marine ecosystems and forests as a result of stratospheric ozone loss. These effects should decline as ozone-destroying chemicals are phased out and the springtime ozone layer recovers. This will take decades, however; and it will be necessary to continue monitoring ozone loss, as some of the compounds that have replaced the ozone-damaging chemicals are also ozone damaging or have other negative environmental effects. Despite ongoing concerns, the international treaty protecting the ozone layer, the Montreal Protocol, has been a singular success in the environmental movement. The recognition of this massive problem came about because a graduate student performed novel calculations and discovered a risk that more established scientists had assumed was not there.

Climate Change

Climate is changing; that is certain. Glaciers are disappearing and polar ice caps are melting at an unprecedented rate. Winters are shorter and extreme weather events are becoming more normal: Catastrophic floods, record-breaking heat waves, and unprecedented hurricane activity are all more common than they were in past decades or centuries. Plants and animals are changing their ranges to find more comfortable conditions. These transformations have been attributed to **global warming**, which stems from the buildup of greenhouse gases in the atmosphere due to such human activities as fossil-fuel burning and to the destruction of forests. Solving the climate change problem will require new technologies and perhaps some sacrifices.

CLIMATE CHANGE THROUGH TIME

Climate varies geographically, between continents, within continents, even on opposite sides of mountains or lakes. Climate also varies temporally—that is, with time. Climate has changed throughout Earth history; there have been hot, wet periods, such as when the dinosaurs ruled the planet, and ice ages when much of the land surface was covered by glaciers. Just 18,000 years ago, at the peak of the last ice age, New York City and nearly everything north of that latitude was shrouded in ice. Since then, average global temperature has risen 7°F (4°C), and glaciers are only found in high mountains and in the polar regions. Each year, the rate at which glaciers and ice caps are shrinking is increasing.

Large temperature increases are no surprise: During the warm intervals within the last set of ice ages, known as interglacial periods, global temperature was even higher than it is today. What is a surprise is this: Since the beginning of the Industrial Revolution, about 150 years ago, the rate of temperature increase has accelerated dramatically. It took 18,000 years for global temperature to rise 6°F (3.4°C), but it took only a century (1906 to 2005) for global temperature to rise another 1.3°F (0.74°C).

Although the idea was once controversial, nearly all climate scientists now attribute this accelerated temperature increase to the rise in atmospheric greenhouse gases due to the widespread burning of fossil fuels and biomass. Many of the world's politicians are recognizing the importance of climate change. Former British prime minister Tony Blair has called climate change the world's greatest environmental challenge. Blair expressed his ideas in the forward of the 2006 book, *Avoiding Dangerous Climate Change*: "It is now plain that the emission of greenhouse gases, associated with industrialization and economic growth from a world population that has increased six-fold in 200 years, is causing global warming at a rate that is unsustainable." At this time, rapid changes in the environment are causing other powerful world leaders to come around to the idea as well.

GREENHOUSE GASES AND GLOBAL WARMING

As was described in Chapter 1, greenhouse gases trap heat and insulate the Earth, which moderates global climate. Greenhouse gases include carbon dioxide (CO_2), water vapor, ozone (O_3), methane, nitrous oxide, and synthetic gases such as chlorofluorocarbons (CFCs). All greenhouse gases do not have the same heat-trapping ability. For example, one CFC molecule traps as much heat as 10,000 CO_2 molecules; methane traps about 23 times as much heat as CO_2. Since water vapor and CO_2 are so much more abundant than the other gases, they have a much greater impact on global temperature.

Natural events—volcanic processes, the decay and burning of organic matter, and respiration by animals—are constantly adding greenhouse gases to the atmosphere. Greenhouse gases are also constantly being removed. CO_2, for example, is absorbed by water, so the oceans contain an enormous amount of the gas. CO_2 is also stored in plant and animal tissue, and forests contain large reservoirs of CO_2. As plants and animals die and their remains settle deep in the Earth, fossil fuels sequester their CO_2. The removal of greenhouse gases from the atmosphere keeps the planet from overheating.

Now some of this stored CO_2 is being released back into the atmosphere. Although people have been burning wood and coal to meet their energy needs for thousands of years, fossil-fuel usage has increased astronomically since the Industrial Revolution. In addition, slash-and-burn agriculture in the tropics releases the CO_2 stored in rainforests. At present, there is 27% more CO_2 in the atmosphere than there was 100 years ago, with 65% of that increase taking place since 1958. The rate of CO_2 increase is growing: There was 36% more CO_2 added annually, on average, in the 10 years from 1995 to 2005 than in the 1960 to 2005 average.

Other greenhouse gas levels are rising as well. Methane has increased nearly 250% since pre-industrial times and is at more than twice the highest measured value of the last 650,000 years. Methane growth is due to the increases in livestock, rice production, and the incomplete burning of rainforest materials for creating farmland that higher human populations require. Levels of CFCs, compounds that were unknown before 1928, have risen tremendously in recent decades, although they are now being phased out. Concentrations of tropospheric ozone have more than doubled since 1976.

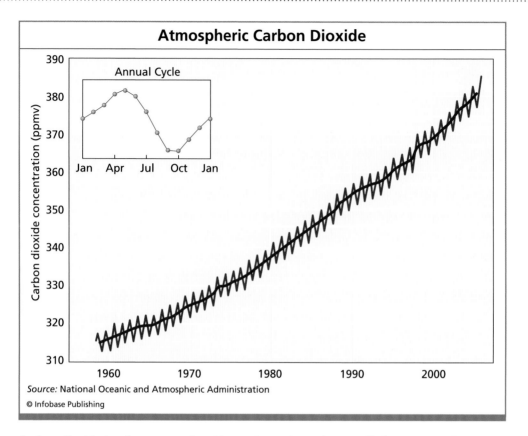

Carbon dioxide levels measured on Mauna Loa volcano in Hawaii shows a steady increase between 1958 and 2005. The annual cycle reflects the absorption of carbon in the spring and summer as plants grow, and the release of carbon in the fall and winter as they decay.

Adding greenhouse gases to the atmosphere is like throwing a blanket on the Earth. The last half century has been the warmest in at least the past 500 years and likely the past 1,300 years. The 11 years from 1995 to 2006 were among the 12 warmest since 1850. The last time temperatures were significantly warmer for a sustained period was in the last interglacial period, which was about 125,000 years ago. If no curb is placed on greenhouse gas emissions, those emissions will continue to grow. The question is not if increases in atmospheric greenhouse gases will cause global temperature to continue to rise, but how much and how fast.

THE CONSEQUENCES OF CLIMATE CHANGE

To attempt to determine the effects of global warming on the planet, climate scientists construct models of future climate. But climate is a complex system, with many variables, which makes this a difficult task. Some models forecast extreme alterations in impending climate and some are more conservative. Models predict that if greenhouse gas emissions continue at constant rates, average global temperature will increase by 3.6° to 8.1°F (2° to 4.5°C) by 2100. These temperature increases will not be uniform; the Southern Hemisphere will warm less than the Northern Hemisphere since the high coverage of ocean water south of the equator absorbs more heat. A far greater temperature increase, perhaps 14° to 18°F (8° to 10°C), is slated to occur at the poles.

While climate change on the Earth is not unusual, the effects of rapid warming of the planet may be catastrophic to social and environmental systems. An increase of 3.5°F (2°C) is predicted to threaten water supplies in Latin America and food yields in Asia, and to increase extreme weather conditions in the Caribbean. Rising temperatures will melt glaciers and polar ice caps, resulting in an abrupt sea level rise. Sea level could rise 2.1 feet (65 cm) by the end of the century. Coastal regions—where about one-third of the world's population lives and an enormous amount of economic infrastructure is concentrated—will flood. Rising sea level will destroy coral reefs, accelerate coastal erosion, and increase salinity to coastal groundwater systems.

Plant and animal species seeking cooler temperatures will need to move poleward 60 to 90 miles (100 to 150 km) or upward 500 feet (150 m) for each 1.8°F (1°C) rise in global temperature. **Biodiversity**, the number of species in a given habitat, will decline because plants and animals will not be able to migrate that rapidly. Native species will be driven out by more heat-tolerant nonnative species.

Climate models predict that a warmer Earth will have more extreme weather. There are two reasons for this: Many weather events are caused by high temperatures, and warm air can hold more moisture than cool air, thus allowing greater chance for precipitation. Nearly all land areas will experience higher minimum temperatures, with fewer

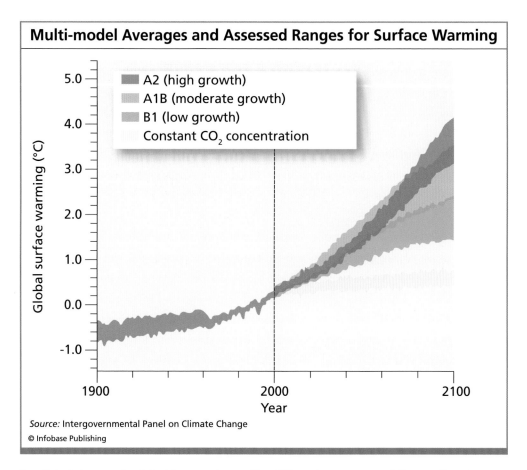

Multi-model Averages and Assessed Ranges for Surface Warming

Source: Intergovernmental Panel on Climate Change
© Infobase Publishing

Predicted changes in global temperatures. The different ranges reveal the predicted temperature rises of different modeling scenarios. The A2 model describes continuously increasing population, regional economic development, and slow adoption of efficient and new technological changes. The A1B model describes rapid economic growth, global population peaking in mid-century, and the rapid introduction of new and more effective technologies. The B1 model resembles A1B except for very rapid adoption of clean and resource-efficient technologies. The yellow band shows temperature increases if no greenhouse gases were added after 2000.

A heat wave over Chicago in 1995. Smog and heat are trapped beneath a deadly inversion. *(Gary Braasch from the book* Earth Under Fire: How Global Warming Is Changing the World, *University of California Press, 2007)*

cold days and fewer cold snaps, and higher maximum temperatures, with more hot days and more heat waves. Warm regions will endure the greatest increase in heat wave severity, but even temperate regions will experience an increase in heat wave severity. In models of climate for the years 2080 to 2099, Chicago, Illinois, will have 25% more heat waves, and Paris, France, will have 31% more heat waves. The heat wave duration will increase 64% in Chicago and 52% in Paris. Precipitation events will also increase, although summers will be a lot drier in some regions and droughts will become more common.

An increase in sea surface temperatures will bring about more El Niño events, and regions will experience more floods or more droughts as a result. The Asian monsoon will likely become more unpredictable.

Drought will make many marginal regions uninhabitable. Precipitation will increase globally, but some regions may have decreases. Storms will become more frequent due to an increase in global air and sea temperatures. Already there has been a 20% increase in blizzards and heavy rainstorms in the United States since 1900, and the total amount of winter precipitation is up 10%.

Since warmer air temperatures will also increase sea surface temperatures, it would seem likely that global warming will bring about an increase in the number of hurricanes. Yet another factor is likely to come into play. Global warming may increase the wind shear between the lower and upper atmosphere, which would cause many storms to be decapitated before they have a chance to mature. The hurricanes that do form, however, are likely to be more intense and to produce more rain. A 2005 study reported in *Nature*, by Kerry Emanuel of the Massachusetts Institute of Technology indicates that, by at least one measure, hurricanes have already almost doubled in intensity over the last 30 years. According to Professor Emanuel, "The large upswing in the last decade is unprecedented, and probably reflects the effect of global warming."

A model of future events shows that by 2080, each hurricane will be approximately one-half point higher on the Saffir-Simpson scale than the current average, resulting in a 20% increase in rainfall. A summary of 1,200 simulations published in the *Journal of Climate* in April 2004 showed that rising levels of greenhouse gases could triple the number of Category 5 hurricanes. Professor Emmanuel writes, "My results suggest that future warming may lead to . . . a substantial increase in hurricane-related losses in the 21st century."

Any rise in sea level due to melting ice caps will compound the destruction of a hurricane's storm surge, high tides, and strong waves. The Federal Emergency Management Agency (FEMA) found that a one-foot rise in sea levels would increase flood damage by 36% to 58%. Higher ocean temperatures may also alter the hurricane track, bringing more hurricanes through the Caribbean and onto the eastern United States seaboard.

Some models predict that the midwestern United States will be too dry to support agriculture, and the North American bread basket will move into Canada. Similar changes will occur all over the world, resulting in a total loss of current cropland of 10% to 50% and a decline in the global yield of key food crops from 10% to 70%. As temperatures warm, tropical and subtropical insects will expand their ranges, spreading tropical diseases such as malaria, encephalitis, yellow fever, and dengue fever. Heat-related diseases and deaths will increase.

THE KYOTO PROTOCOL

The Kyoto Protocol is designed to lessen the effects of climate change by lowering emissions of greenhouse gases. Like the Montreal Protocol, it attempts to solve an environmental problem by having the countries of the world agree to limit the production of environmentally damaging compounds. Kyoto was ratified in 2004 after several years of debates. Of the 130 countries that signed, 36 were industrialized nations that agreed to cut back their CO_2 emissions to at least 5% below 1990 levels by 2012. In 1990, these nations produced 55% of the total emissions put out by the industrialized countries. Similar to cap-and-trade programs, the treaty allows the signatories to trade credits among themselves and to earn credits by assisting other nations with their emissions reductions; for example, by preserving forests in developing nations.

Unfortunately, Kyoto has many flaws, the most glaring being the fact that some countries are not bound by it. The United States, which emits the most greenhouse gases of any country—21% of the world's total in 2000—refused to sign and will engage in only voluntary cutbacks. The number-two emitter, China, released 15% of emissions in 2000, yet it and other developing nations are exempt to protect their growing economies. It is likely that the emissions of the developing world will exceed those of the developed world in several decades. Exempting them is ignoring an enormous source of greenhouse gases. One climate model shows that more than 40 times the emissions reductions required by the Kyoto Protocol would be needed to prevent atmospheric CO_2 concentrations from doubling during this century.

MAKING A DIFFERENCE ON CLIMATE CHANGE

Reducing greenhouse gas emissions enough to curb the growth in the planet's warming trend will require action from individuals and from governments at all levels: local, regional, national, and international. The Union of Concerned Scientists has published a set of actions that individuals can take to reduce their contribution to global warming. Many of these actions are similar to those suggested in Chapter 11 for reducing air pollution, since the emissions come largely from the same sources. Most importantly, people must use less gasoline, natural gas, oil, and electricity. Because the bulk of energy use is related to transportation, these choices are especially important.

Some valuable actions individuals can take to reduce their contribution to global warming are:

⊕ Buy only fuel-efficient vehicles. Every gallon of gasoline burned emits 20 pounds (9.1 kilograms) of CO_2 and many other pollutants.

⊕ Try to live near work, school, and other activities to reduce the amount of driving.

⊕ Reduce gasoline consumption by carpooling, taking mass transit, walking, or riding a bike.

⊕ Buy energy-efficient appliances by looking for the EPA's Energy Star.

⊕ Determine ways in which every member of the family can reduce energy use. Even small changes can help: Boil only the amount of water needed; turn off TVs, computers, and lights when not in use; take showers instead of baths.

⊕ Plant a tree (or two) to absorb CO_2 emissions.

Some actions people can take within their communities are:

⊕ Encourage energy efficiency and the use of alternative energy sources in public buildings.

⊕ Request amenities for bicyclists: the installation of bike racks in public areas and the construction of bike lanes.

- Promote carpooling lanes and plans.
- Encourage utilities to promote energy efficiency and alternative energy sources.

Ways individuals can encourage action by the United States include:

- Monitor press coverage of global warming:
  - Stress the need for the United States to become a leader in reducing greenhouse emissions.
  - Respond to stories or letters that diminish the seriousness of climate change.
- Contact federal officials—the president, senators, and congressional representatives—to encourage them to take action on reducing greenhouse gas emissions.
- Contact state officials—the governor, state legislators, and public-utility regulators—to promote energy efficiency, the development of alternative energy sources, and mass transportation.
- Encourage all government leaders to urge industry to reduce greenhouse gas emissions.

In the long term, even more action will be needed to rein in global warming. Money is often an effective motivator, and many economists agree that a good way to encourage energy conservation is through taxes. A surcharge placed on the use of energy sources that release CO_2 into the atmosphere is a **carbon tax**. Such a tax can be added to the pump price of gasoline or onto the electrical bill for households and businesses that rely on coal-fired power plants, for example. Consumers thus pay more tax if they use more energy, and less tax if they use less energy. The tax gives people an economic incentive to be more energy efficient: to drive less, purchase fuel-efficient vehicles, buy energy-efficient appliances, and keep the heat turned down. The money collected can be used for research on alternative fuels and to develop mass transit systems, among other things. Because a carbon tax gives people and companies a financial incentive to conserve energy, industry has an incentive to produce more energy-efficient vehicles and appliances.

Decreasing energy use is not the only way to decrease greenhouse gas emissions. Plants absorb CO_2 and are an important reservoir for sequestering the gas. Plant growth should be encouraged and burning forests should be especially discouraged. Since much of this activity, such as slash-and-burn agriculture, takes place in developing countries, the situation is politically difficult. The developed nations must work with these countries to help them become more self-sufficient without resorting to the destruction of their forests. Consumers in the developed world can decrease their consumption of paper, wood, and beef from fast food outlets. In addition, consumers can research the environmental history of products and the companies that make them.

WRAP-UP

Rising temperatures have been a feature of the Earth's climate since the end of the last ice age, but the rise has accelerated in the past few decades. The cause is rising levels in the atmosphere of CO_2 and other greenhouse gases that are emitted by human activities such as fossil fuel and forest burning. Climate scientists suggest that something must be done to reduce greenhouse gas emissions and it must be done soon. A carbon tax placed on energy use would increase energy efficiency and encourage the research and development of alternative technologies. Scientists also suggest that all governments must band together to require emissions reductions in a way similar to the Kyoto Protocol, but with more drastic cuts in greenhouse gases and with the inclusion of the largest emitters and the developing nations.

Conclusion

The Earth and its atmosphere face many difficult problems—problems brought about by human activities. Some of these troubles have already been dealt with in positive ways. Phasing out ozone-depleting chemicals has reversed the increase in the size of the ozone hole and may lead to its near repair within several decades. Pollution-control devices have cleansed the air of some harmful pollutants. Concentrations of the six major pollutants—ozone, particulates, sulfur dioxide, nitrogen dioxide, carbon monoxide, and lead—have declined in much of the developed world, and the air over many cities is much cleaner than it was a few decades ago. Pollution-control devices also diminish the pollutants that bring about acid rain.

Many Americans still breathe dirty air, and many lakes and streams suffer from high acidity. As Earth's population grows, and there are more cars and industries, more drastic solutions will be needed so that air quality can continue to improve. Economic incentives to reduce energy use and to advance and expand the use of pollutant-reducing technologies must be increased. Incentives can target industry,

Smog over the northeastern United States. *(NASA /MODIS Rapid Response Team /Goddard Space Flight Center)*

small businesses, and even individuals, who can be motivated economically to purchase less-polluting cars or to use public transportation. Where incentives are not enough, pollutant emission restrictions will need to be discussed and implemented. Controlling smog and acid rain are necessary to decrease the problems associated with both human and environmental health.

By many measures, the situation in the developed world is improving; but the developing nations are becoming more polluted as their populations increase and their standards of living improve. Rising population and standards of living increase consumption and its by-product, pollution. While developing economies are loathe to take actions that may slow their growth, long-term environmental and human health concerns must be taken into account as part of the real cost of becoming a developed society.

Climate change is a much more complex issue than air pollution. The greenhouse gases that cause it are an important part of the atmosphere, and most seem innocuous. Carbon dioxide is essential for life on the Earth, yet the swell in CO_2 levels as increasing amounts of fossil fuels are burned correlates directly with the rise of average global temperature. Climate scientists and an increasing number of politicians worldwide say that this relationship is causative: Fossil fuel burning has increased levels of atmospheric CO_2, and this increase has increased global temperature. Biomass burning has also contributed to the increase in atmospheric CO_2 since plants release the CO_2 they have absorbed back into the atmosphere, and once burned, those plants are no longer available to absorb more CO_2. Large increases in other greenhouse gases, such as methane and CFCs, have also played a role.

Modern society is built on the energy that fossil fuel burning provides. While it is simple to see that reducing CO_2 and other greenhouse gas emissions would stop the globe from warming so much and so fast, doing this on a large enough scale to make a difference would take a hefty commitment by governments and individuals to reduce or eliminate the use of fossil fuels. Such a change would require a change in attitudes about alternative energy sources. Less centralized and smaller scale energy sources, such as solar and wind power, need to be encouraged and employed. Technologies that decrease greenhouse gas emissions from fossil-fuel burning vehicles and plants will need to be developed and utilized globally.

Before large changes in society can be made, people will need to make changes in their attitudes. Everyone should gain knowledge of the science behind the problems facing us and make informed decisions regarding lifestyle choices. Individuals need to do what they can by reducing the amount of driving they do and by voting with their pocketbooks—buying only necessary and environmentally friendly (or at least less-damaging) products. Most importantly, people must bring their knowledge of these topics to bear when they make political decisions. They must support candidates who are more likely to implement policies that value the long-term future of the planet and who will work toward the adoption of those policies in the United States and around the world.

With education in the needs of the world and its environment, coupled with hope and enthusiasm, young people will play a major role in implementing change. The path the world is on can be turned, incrementally and completely, with knowledge, dedication, and determination.

Glossary

acid precipitation Any precipitation—rain, snow, fog or dew—with a pH of less than 5.0.

acid rain Rainfall with a pH of less than 5.0; acid rain is a type of acid precipitation.

advection The horizontal movement of material in a convection cell; horizontal movement of air is known as wind.

advection fog Fog formed from warm, wet air blowing over cold water. They are blown inland by onshore breezes.

aerosols Solid or liquid pollutants that are small enough to stay suspended in the air. They are generally nontoxic but can seriously reduce visibility.

air mass A large body of air in which temperature and humidity are similar, although they differ with altitude.

air pollution Contamination of the air by particulates and toxic gases in concentrations that can endanger human and environmental health. Also known as smog.

albedo The amount of light that reflects back off a surface; snow and ice have high albedo, mud has low albedo.

alkaline Solutions with hydroxyl ions (OH-) that are acrid to the taste. Acidic and alkaline solutions neutralize to form salts.

altitude Vertical distance above or below mean sea level.

anticyclone Winds spiraling outward from a high pressure zone; the opposite of a cyclone.

asthma   A chronic inflammatory respiratory disease characterized by periodic attacks of wheezing, shortness of breath, and a tight feeling in the chest.

atherosclerosis   The deposition of fatty deposits in the arteries.

atmosphere   The gases surrounding a planet or a moon.

atmospheric pressure   The force of the air over any point on a planet's surface area; also known as air pressure.

aurora   A display of lights of many colors caused by the collision of electrically charged particles from the solar wind with gases in the atmosphere. In the Northern Hemisphere, the phenomenon is known as the aurora borealis, or northern lights; in the Southern Hemisphere it is known as the aurora australis, or southern lights.

baghouse   An enclosed structure that uses filter bags to help remove pollutants from emissions gases in the same way a vacuum cleaner removes dirt from floors.

bioaccumulation   The accumulation of toxic substances within living organisms.

biodiversity   The number of plant and animal species in a given habitat.

biomass   The amount of living material in a given habitat.

buffering capacity   The ability of a solution to resist changes in pH.

cancer   A group of more than 100 distinct diseases that are typified by the uncontrolled growth of abnormal cells in the body.

carbon tax   A tax placed on emissions of carbon dioxide from energy sources such as power plants and motor vehicles that would increase the price of energy to take into account the true costs of the commodity. The money generated would increase energy efficiency and would provide incentive to increase research and development into alternative energy sources.

carcinogen   A substance that causes cancer. Carcinogens affect people with a genetic predisposition for getting the disease more than those who do not, except in cases of extreme exposure to the carcinogen.

catalyst   A substance that can cause a change in the rate of a chemical reaction without being consumed in the reaction.

catalytic converter   A device found on modern motor vehicles that uses a catalyst to reduce and oxidize three pollutants: carbon monoxide, nitrogen oxides, and volatile organic compounds.

centrifugal forces   Forces moving or directed outward from a center.

Chinook winds   Low pressure on the leeward side of a mountain range that draws warm, dry air over the mountains.

chlorofluorocarbon (CFC)   An anthropogenic gas that rises into the stratosphere and breaks down ozone.

clean coal   Coal that has undergone gasification to clean it of pollutants before it is burned.

cold front   A front in which cold air pushes warm air upward.

condensation   The change in state of a substance from a gas to a liquid.

condensation level   The altitude in the atmosphere at which air reaches its dew point and clouds can form.

conduction   The transfer of heat by the molecular motion of adjacent particles.

convection   The transfer of heat by the movement of currents.

convection cell   A current in which warm material rises, then moves sideways and cools. When it becomes dense enough, it sinks. It then moves back to where it began and warms.

Coriolis effect   The tendency of a moving object to appear to move sideways due to the Earth's rotation.

cyclone   (1) A system of winds rotating around a low pressure center. (2) An antipollution device in which gas emissions are spun around a cylinder so fast that centrifugal forces move the particles to the outer wall where they can be collected.

density   Mass of a substance per unit volume.

dew point   The temperature at which air is so saturated with water vapor that the vapor begins to condense.

dioxin   Chlorinated hydrocarbon that is a byproduct of other processes but is not manufactured itself.

ecosystem   The interrelationships of the plants and animals of a region and the raw materials that they need to live.

electromagnetic waves   The form in which radiation travels; these waves have electrical and magnetic properties.

electronic precipitators   Pollutant-collecting devices in which particles suspended in very hot gases are attracted by static electricity and then removed.

El Niño   A temporary warming of the Pacific Ocean that influences global weather patterns.

evaporative cooling   The cooling that takes place when water changes its state from a liquid to a gas.

evaporation   The change of state of a substance from a liquid to a gas, such as the change from liquid water to water vapor.

evapotranspiration   The loss of water by evaporation in plants.

evolution   Change through time. In science, evolution usually refers to organic evolution, which is the change in organisms caused by the process of natural selection.

fossil fuels   Ancient plants that have decayed and been transformed into usable fuels, especially coal and petroleum. These fuels can be thought of as stored ancient sunshine.

front   The meeting place of two air masses; a front will be stormy if the air masses have very different characteristics of temperature and humidity.

fuel cell   An energy cell in which chemical energy is converted into electrical energy.

gasification   A technology used to produce clean coal for power plants.

global warming   The worldwide rising of average global temperature; the term usually refers to the temperature increases that have taken place in the past one-and-a-half centuries.

greenhouse effect   The trapping of heat that is radiated from the Earth. Without the greenhouse effect, Earth's average temperature would be much lower.

greenhouse gases   Gases that absorb heat radiated from the Earth. They include carbon dioxide, methane, ozone, nitrous oxide, and chlorofluorocarbons.

gyre Major ocean currents that travel in a loop; gyres are large and move water around in large portions of the ocean basins. They rotate clockwise in the Northern Hemisphere and counterclockwise in the Southern.

heat index (HI) A measure of the effects of high temperatures coupled with humidity.

high pressure zone A location in which relatively cool, dense air is sinking.

hybrid vehicle A fuel-efficient vehicle that runs on a small, internal combustion engine, an electric motor, and a rechargeable battery.

humidity The amount of water vapor in the air.

inert Word used to describe an element that does not react chemically with other elements or compounds.

infrared Electromagnetic energy with wavelengths longer than red; infrared energy is also known as heat and is found at about 50 miles (80 km) above the Earth's surface.

input The amount of a substance that enters a system.

insulation The use of materials to inhibit the conduction of heat or electricity.

jet streams Swift air currents traveling between air masses of very different temperature. The major ones are the polar jet streams and the subtropical jet streams.

kinetic energy The energy an object holds because it is in motion.

land breeze Cool air from land that blows over the warmer ocean at night or in winter.

La Niña The reverse of an El Niño, in which the surface of the Pacific Ocean off South America is especially cold.

latent heat The energy absorbed or released when a substance changes state from a solid to a liquid or a liquid to a gas.

latitude The angular distance of any point on the surface of the Earth, north or south of the equator.

lead A metal—once added to gasoline, paint, pipes, and other materials—that is toxic even in tiny doses.

lime   Calcium carbonate; carbonates can neutralize acids.

low pressure zone   A location in which relatively warm, less dense air is rising.

melanoma   Skin cancer that targets the deeper layers of skin; melanoma is the most serious skin cancer and results in the vast majority of skin cancer fatalities.

mercury   The only metal that is liquid at room temperature. It is toxic in liquid form and also as a salt or an organic compound.

methane   A hydrocarbon gas (CH4) that is the major component of natural gas. Methane is also a natural component of the atmosphere and a greenhouse gas.

microburst   Horizontal wind movement on the ground below a severe thunderstorm.

mid-latitude cyclones   Cyclones that occur in the middle latitudes. They are responsible for much of the planet's unsettled weather.

mirage   An optical illusion in which an observer sees a nonexistent object, scene, or, most often, body of water in the distance.

monsoon   A seasonally shifting wind pattern between a warm continent and relatively cool ocean in the summer and the reverse in the winter. Summer monsoons often bring abundant rain.

mountain breeze   Air over a mountain slope that cools and sinks, bringing higher air downhill into the valley.

nitrous oxides   NO and NO_2, referred to collectively as NO_x. They are natural components of the atmosphere and are greenhouse gases.

noble gases   Colorless, odorless, tasteless, and almost entirely chemically inert gases that include argon, neon, helium, and xenon.

Nor'easter (northeaster)   A mid-latitude cyclone or northeastern storm that dumps snow, rain, and ice on the mid-Atlantic and New England states each winter.

noctilucent clouds   Stratospheric clouds composed of tiny ice crystals.

NO_x   The nitrous oxides NO and NO_2.

occluded front   A front in which a warm air mass is pushed up over a cold air mass.

output   The amount of a substance that leaves a system.

oxidation   The process that takes place when an element combines with oxygen. An example is the formation of rust.

ozone   A molecule composed of three oxygen atoms and symbolized as O_3. Ozone is a pollutant in the lower atmosphere, but in the upper atmosphere, it protects us from the Sun's deadly ultraviolet radiation.

ozone hole   A "hole" in the ozone layer where ozone concentrations are diminished; usually referring to the Antarctic ozone hole.

ozone layer   The layer, located at between 9 and 19 miles (15 to 30 km) up in the stratosphere, in which ozone is concentrated. The ozone layer shields us from the Sun's ultraviolet radiation.

particulates   Solid or liquid pollutants that are small enough to stay suspended in the air. They are generally nontoxic but can seriously reduce visibility.

pH   Numbers from 0 to 14 that express the acidity or alkalinity of a solution. On the pH scale, 7 is neutral, with lower numbers indicating acid and higher numbers indicating base. The most extreme numbers are the most extreme solutions.

photochemical smog   Air pollution that forms when sunlight facilitates the chemical reaction of pollutants such as nitrogen oxides and hydrocarbons.

photosynthesis   The process by which plants use carbon dioxide and water to produce sugar and oxygen. The simplified chemical reaction is $6CO_2 + 12H_2O + \text{solar energy} = C_6H_{12}O_6 + 6O_2 + 6H_2O$.

phytoplankton   Microscopic plants found at the surface of the ocean; they are the planet's single greatest source of oxygen.

plankton   Tiny plants (phytoplankton) and animals (zooplankton) that live at the sea surface and form the lower levels of the ocean's food web.

polar front   The meeting zone of cold, dry polar air and relatively warm equatorial air at about the latitudes of 50°N and 50°S.

polar stratospheric clouds (PSCs)   Stratospheric clouds that are composed of water and nitric acid; they are necessary for the breakdown of chlorofluorocarbons in the atmosphere.

pollutants Artificial impurities that are found in the atmosphere. They include nitrogen dioxide (NO_2), sulfur dioxide (SO_2), carbon monoxide (CO), hydrocarbons, and ozone (O_3).

precipitation The process by which condensed moisture falls to the ground as rain, sleet, hail, snow, frost, or dew.

primary pollutants Impurities that enter the air directly, such as from a smokestack or tailpipe.

radiation The emission and transmission of energy through space or material; also the radiated energy itself.

radiation fog Fog originating when warm moist air is cooled below its dew point by the ground.

rain shadow The relatively dry conditions found on the leeward side of a mountain or mountain range.

reflection The return of a wave from a surface.

refraction The bending of a light beam as it moves from one medium to another.

respiration The process by which an organism exchanges gases with the environment. Note that in the reaction, sugar and CO_2 are converted into oxygen and water with the release of energy: $C_6H_{12}O_6 + 6O_2 = 6CO_2 + 6H_2O$ + released energy.

scattering The diffusion or deflection of light as it strikes particles.

scrubbers Air-cleansing devices used in smokestacks for removing particulates, SO_2, hydrogen sulfide, and other pollutants during the combustion of coal and the processing of petroleum.

sea breeze Cool ocean air that blows over the warmer land on summer afternoons.

secondary pollutants Pollutants that are the result of a chemical reaction between a primary pollutant and some other component of air, such as water vapor or another pollutant.

slash-and-burn agriculture In the tropics, rain forest plants are slashed down and then burned to clear the land for agriculture.

smog Vernacular term for air pollution; a contraction of smoke and fog.

solar wind   High-speed protons and electrons that travel outward from the Sun through the solar system.

specific heat   The amount of energy needed to raise the temperature of 1 gram of material by 1.8°F (1°C).

squall line   A line of thunderstorms, usually hundreds of miles long, that forms at the edge of a cold front.

stationary front   A front in which the air sits over a region and does not move.

steam fog   A fog that forms when cool air moves over a lake that has retained some of its summer heat.

stoma   Small pores in plant leaves through which gases are exchanged.

storm surge   Abnormally high sea level due to water being raised up by low pressure and by water being blown up against land.

stratosphere   The upper atmosphere, which rises from the troposphere to about 30 miles (45 km) up. The stratosphere contains the ozone layer.

temperature gradient   The change in the temperature of a material along its length (or altitude when measuring the temperature gradient of the atmosphere.)

temperature inversion   An increase in the air temperature of the atmosphere that occurs with an increase in altitude.

temperature range   The difference in high and low temperature at a particular location during a specified time period, such as a day or a year.

topography   The elevations and depressions of the ground surface.

troposphere   The lowest layer of Earth's atmosphere, rising from sea level to about 6 miles (11 km).

ultraviolet radiation (UV)   Short-wave, high-energy radiation along the electromagnetic spectrum. UV comes in three types: UVA, UVB, and UVC, with UVC having the shortest wavelength and therefore being the most dangerous type.

upslope fog   Fog that forms when warm, humid air travels up a hillside and cools below its dew point.

urban heat island effect   A phenomenon in which urban areas have higher temperatures than nearby rural areas due to the urban areas' absorption of sunlight and release of heat by their ground coverings (such as concrete) and to the urban areas' collection of waste heat.

valley breeze   Air warmed on mountain slopes that rises and sucks cool valley air upward.

volatile organic compounds (VOCs)   Mostly man-made chemicals that enter the atmosphere primarily by evaporation and that result from the manufacture, refining, and incomplete burning of petroleum, among many other substances.

warm front   A weather front in which warm air overtakes the position of cold air.

water vapor   Water (H_2O) in its gaseous state.

wavelength   The distance from crest to crest or trough to trough in a wave.

westerly winds or westerlies   Winds that move from west to east between the approximate latitudes 30° to 50° north and south of the equator.

zooplankton   Tiny marine animals that are unable to swim on their own and drift with the currents.

Further Reading

Allaby, Michael. *How Weather Works*. Washington, D.C.: Readers Digest, 1999.

ANU Reporter. "Hell's Milder Side." Australia National University, 2005. Available online. http://info.anu.edu.au/mac/Newsletters_and_Journals/ANU_Reporter/098PP_2005/_003_Winter/_hell's_milder_side.asp. Accessed March 16, 2007.

Athanasiou, Tom, and Paul Baer. *Dead Heat: Globalization and Global Warming*. New York: Seven Stories Press, 2002.

Ayers, Harvard, Charles E. Little, and Jenny Hager. *An Appalachian Tragedy: Air Pollution and Tree Death in the Eastern Forests of North America*. San Francisco: Sierra Club Books, 1998.

Burt, Christopher, and Mark Stroud. *Extreme Weather: A Guide and Record Book*. New York: W.W. Norton and Company, 2004.

Center for International Earth Science Information Network (CIESIN) of Columbia University. "Ozone Depletion and Global Environmental Change." Available online. http://www.ciesin.org/TG/OZ/oz-home.html. Accessed March 16, 2007.

Centre of Atmospheric Science, University of Cambridge. "The Ozone Hole Tour." Available online. http://www.atm.ch.cam.ac.uk/tour/. Accessed March 16, 2007.

Dorschner, Cheryl. "Acid Rain Damage Far Worse Than Previously Believed, USA." *Medical News Today* (July, 2005). Available online. URL: http://www.medicalnewstoday.com/medicalnews.php?newsid=27550. Accessed March 16, 2007.

Drye, William. *Storm of the Century: The Labor Day Hurricane of 1935*. Washington, D.C.: National Geographic, 2002.

Emanuel, K.A. *Divine Wind: The History and Science of Hurricanes.* New York: Oxford University Press, 2005.

———. "Increasing Destructiveness of Tropical Cyclones over the Past 30 Years." *Nature* 436 (August, 2005): pp. 686–688.

Environment Canada. "Acid Rain." Available online. URL: http://www.ec.gc.ca/acidrain/. Accessed March 16, 2007.

Environmental Defense. "Scorecard: The Pollution Information Site." Available online. URL: http://www.scorecard.org/. Accessed March 16, 2007.

Environmental Protection Agency (EPA). "Energy Star." Available online. URL: http://www.energystar.gov. Accessed March 16, 2007.

———. "Climate Change." Available online. URL: http://www.epa.gov/climatechange/index.html. Accessed March 16, 2007.

———. "Green Vehicle Guide." Available online. URL: http://www.epa.gov/autoemissions/. Accessed March 16, 2007.

———. "Heat Island Effect." Available online. URL: http://www.epa.gov/heatisland/. Accessed March 16, 2007.

———. "Ozone Depletion." Available online. http://www.epa.gov/docs/ozone/. Accessed March 16, 2007.

———. "Toxic Air Pollutants." Available online. http://www.epa.gov/air/toxicair/index.html. Accessed March 16, 2007.

Flannery, Tim. *The Weather Makers: How Man Is Changing Climate and What It Means for Life on Earth.* New York: Atlantic Monthly Press, 2006.

Gore, Al. *An Inconvenient Truth: The Planetary Emergency of Global Warming and What We Can Do About It.* New York: Rodale, 2006.

Houghton, John. *Global Warming: The Complete Briefing.* Cambridge, U.K.: Cambridge University Press, 2004.

Huler, Scott. *Defining the Wind: The Beaufort Scale and How a 19th-Century Admiral Turned Science into Poetry.* New York: Crown, 2004.

Kay, Jane Holtz. *Asphalt Nation: How the Automobile Took over America, and How We Can Take It Back.* Berkeley: University of California Press, 1998.

Kidd, J. S., and R. A. Kidd. *Into Thin Air: The Problem of Air Pollution.* New York: Facts On File, 1998.

Kitman, Jamie Lincoln. "The Secret History of Lead." *The Nation,* 2000. Available online. http://www.thenation.com/doc.mhtml?i=20000320&c=1&s=kitman. Accessed March 16, 2007.

Kolbert, Elizabeth. *Field Notes from a Catastrophe: Man, Nature, and Climate Change*. New York: Bloomsbury, 2006.

Langholz, Jeffrey, and Kelly Turner. *You Can Prevent Global Warming (and Save Money!): 51 Easy Ways*. New Jersey: Andrews McMeel Publishing, 2003.

Larson, Erik. *Isaac's Storm: A Man, A Time, and the Deadliest Hurricane in History*. New York: Vintage, 2000.

Ludlum, David. *National Audubon Society Field Guide to Weather*. New York: Alfred A. Knopf, 1991.

Medline Plus. "Air Pollution." Available online. URL: http://www.nlm.nih.gov/medlineplus/airpollution.html. Accessed January 4, 2005.

Middlebrook, Ann M., and Margaret A. Tolbert. *Stratospheric Ozone Depletion*. New York: University Science Books, 2000.

National Academy of Sciences. "The Ozone Depletion Phenomenon." Available online. http://www.beyonddiscovery.org/content/view.article.asp?a=73. Accessed March 16, 2007.

National Aeronautics and Atmospheric Administration (NASA). "Earth Observatory." Available online. URL: http://earthobservatory.nasa.gov/Topics/atmosphere.html. Accessed March 16, 2007.

———. "Hurricane Season 2005: Katrina." Available online. URL: http://www.nasa.gov/vision/earth/lookingatearth/h2005_katrina.html. Accessed March 16, 2007.

National Oceanic and Atmospheric Administration (NOAA). "El Niño Theme Page." Available online. URL: http://www.pmel.noaa.gov/tao/elnino/nino-home.html. Accessed March 16, 2007.

———. "Tornadoes." URL: http://www.outlook.noaa.gov/tornadoes/. Accessed March 16, 2007.

Pearce, Fred, and John Gribben. *Global Warming (Essential Science Series)*. New York: Dorling Kindersley Publishing, 2002.

Pidwirny, Michael. "Introduction to the Atmosphere." In *Fundamentals of Physical Geography*. PhysicalGeography.net. Available online. URL: http://www.physicalgeography.net/fundamentals/chapter7.html. Accessed March 16, 2007.

Public Broadcasting Service (PBS) "Surviving the Dust Bowl." *The American Experience*. Available online. URL: http://www.pbs.org/wgbh/amex/dustbowl/. Accessed March 16, 2007.

———— "Tracking El Niño." Available online. URL: http://www.pbs.org/wgbh/nova/elnino/. Accessed March 16, 2007.

Revkin, Andrew. *The North Pole Was Here: Puzzles and Perils at the Top of the World.* Boston: Kingfisher, 2006.

Thornes, J. E., and Gemma Metherell. "The Big Smoke." *Geographical* 74 (2002): pp. 20–27.

Vasquez, Tim. *Storm Chasing Handbook.* Austin, Tex.: Weather Graphics Technologies, 2002.

————. *Weather Forecasting Handbook.* Austin, Tex.: Weather Graphics Technologies, 2002.

Weart, Spencer. *The Discovery of Global Warming.* Cambridge, Mass.: Harvard University Press, 2003.

Winkler, Robert. "Is Acid Rain Killing Off Wood Thrushes?" *National Geographic News* (August, 2002). Available online. URL: http://news.nationalgeographic.com/news/2002/08/0813_020813_acidrain.html. Accessed March 16, 2007.

Wohlforth, Charles. *The Whale and the Supercomputer: On the Northern Front of Climate Change.* New York: North Point Press, 2004.

Web Sites

Alliance to Save Energy
http://www.ase.org
Advice on how to save energy, which results in a healthier economy, a cleaner environment, and greater energy security.

Clouds from Space
http://www.solarviews.com/eng/cloud1.htm
Spectacular cloud images and accompanying descriptions.

Factmonster
http://www.factmonster.com
Online dictionary, encyclopedia, atlas and other helpful aids for finding information on just about anything, from Information Please.

Greenhouse Gas Online

http://www.ghgonline.org

Greenhouse gas science from a greenhouse gas scientist; relates greenhouse gas concentrations to global temperature increases.

Intergovernmental Panel on Climate Change

http://www.ipcc.ch

Access to reports, speeches, graphics, and other materials from the IPCC.

National Climatic Data Center, National Oceanic and Atmospheric Administration (NOAA)

http://lwf.ncdc.noaa.gov/oa/ncdc.html

The world's largest archive of climate data from land-based, marine, satellite, and upper air sources with interpretation and links to many weather topics.

National Drought Mitigation Center, University of Nebraska, Lincoln

http://drought.unl.edu/ndmc/

Background information, case studies, and ways of forecasting drought, including information on the Dust Bowl.

National Severe Storms Laboratory (NSSL), National Oceanic and Atmospheric Administration (NOAA)

http://www.nssl.noaa.gov

About the research and development of predicting and warning the population about an impending severe storm, with a weather room for basic information.

RealClimate

http://www.realclimate.org

Written by working climate scientists for the public and journalists to provide content and context for climate change stories.

Tropical Prediction Center, National Hurricane Center

http://www.nhc.noaa.gov

Predicts and analyzes hurricane data as part of the National Weather Service.

United Nations Environment Programme (UNEP)

http://www.unep.org/ozone/Treaties_and_Ratification/2B_montreal_protocol.asp

Details of the Montreal Protocol and its amendments and adjustments, including the phase-out dates for all chemicals covered.

USAToday.com

http://www.usatoday.com/weather/stormcenter/front.htm

Contains many well-explained, informative pieces on the basics of the atmosphere and weather.

WW2010: The Weather World 2010 Project

http://ww2010.atmos.uiuc.edu/(Gh)/home.rxml

Online instructional modules on meteorology topics including air masses, fronts, clouds, precipitation, El Niño, winds, hurricanes, cyclones, severe storms, and weather forecasting from the University of Illinois.

Index

A

absorption, 23–24, 26–27
acidity, 112
acid precipitations, 113
acid rain
    cap-and-trade programs
        and, 135
    destruction of cultural mate-
        rials and, 119–121
    effects of, 116
    emissions reduction and,
        124
    forests, agriculture and,
        117–119
    freshwater ecosystems and,
        117
    history of, 115
    nitrogen oxides (NOx) and,
        85
    overview of, 110–115
    particulates and, 94–96
    reducing damage from, 121
Acid Rain Program, 134
Acropolis, 120
advection, 17
advection fog, 53
aerosols. *See* particulates
agriculture, 12, 117–119, 154,
    164
air masses, 31–32, 45–47
air pollution. *See also* health
    atmosphere as sink for,
        11–12

biomass burning and, 87–88
chemicals causing, 81–83
costs of, 106, 108–109
external factors affecting,
    92–94
fossil fuels and, 83–86
heat and, 76
history of, 89–91
inversions and, 47
national parks and, 97–99
secondary chemical reac-
    tions and, 86–87
trends in, 124–126
VOCs and, 81, 88–89
Air Pollution Control Act, 91
air pressure. *See* pressure
Air Quality Index (AQI), 128
air quality, 92–94, 126–127
albedo, 23, 28
alkalinity, 112
altitude, 13, 16–19, 48–52
altocumulus clouds, 50
altostratus clouds, 50
amphibians, 117, 118
Andrew (hurricane), 74
animals, 14–15
Antarctic ozone hole, 147,
    149–152
anticyclones, 65–66
approximations, air quality
    and, 126–127
Arctic, ozone depletion in, 150
asthma, 104, 105–106

atherosclerosis, 108
atmosphere, defined, 3
aurora australis, 26
aurora borealis, 26
automobiles. *See* vehicles
Ayres, Chris, 95

B

baghouses, 129
bicycles, 166
Big Smoke event, 89, 102
bioaccumulation, 85–86
biodiversity, 161
biomass burning, 87–88, 126,
    170–171
birds, 118–119
black blizzards, 77
Black Forest, 119
Blair, Tony, 158
British Antarctic Survey, 149
buffering capacity, 116
buildings, 119–120

C

calcium, 118
California, 93, 95–96, 124–
    125, 141–143
California Current, 39, 53
calories, heat and, 8
cancer, 89, 106–108, 125,
    150–152, 154
cap-and-trade programs,
    134–135

Cape Hatteras, 70
carbon cycle, diagram of, 6
carbon dioxide, 5–7, 10, 11–12, 14, 159–160
carbon monoxide, 11, 84, 103, 130–131
carbon taxes, 167–168
carcinogens, 107
cars. *See* vehicles
catalysts, 130
catalytic converters, 130–131
cataracts, 154
certification programs, 136
children, 101–102, 105–106
Chile, 155
China, 82, 96–97, 119, 165
Chinook winds, 54–55
chlorofluorocarbons (CFCs)
    clouds and, 51
    as greenhouse gases, 10, 12
    introduction of, 16
    Montreal Protocol and, 152–153
    ozone loss and, 148–149
    as VOCs, 88
circulation, atmospheric, 28–30
circulation cells. *See* convection cells
cirrocumulus clouds, 49
cirrostratus clouds, 49
cirrus clouds, 48–49
cities, 138–143
Clean Air Acts (England), 90
Clean Air Acts (U.S.), 83, 90–91, 98, 115, 123–124, 133–135
climate
    atmospheric circulation and, 31
    continental position and, 37–38
    latitude and, 35–37
    mountains and, 41–42
    ocean currents and, 38–41

urban vs. rural, 138–141
    weather vs., 45
climate change, 157–158, 161–168, 170–171. *See also* greenhouse gases
clouds, 10–11, 24, 48–53, 141
coal, 83–84, 90, 111–114, 129–130
cold fronts, 47–48
Coliseum, 120
colors, 23–25
composition of atmosphere, 3–7, 14–16
compression, 16–17
condensation, 9, 10–11
condensation level, 51
conduction, 17
convection, 17, 22
convection cells
    atmospheric circulation and, 28–30
    map of, 32
    overview of, 17, 18
    thunderstorms and, 61–62
    wind belts and, 22, 30–31
Coriolis effect, 29–30, 67
costs of air pollution, 106, 108–109
cultural materials, 119–121
cumulonimbus clouds, 61–62
cumulus clouds, 48–49, 50–51, 61
currents, climate and, 38–41
cyclones, 65–68, 68–74, 164
cyclones (equipment), 129

D

density, altitude and, 16–17, 20
dew point, 51
dioxin, 88–89
Doppler radar, 64
downdrafts, 61, 62
drought, 76–78, 163–165
Dust Bowl, 77

E

ecosystems, 57, 97, 117
electromagnetic radiation, 23
electromagnetic waves, 8
electronic precipitators, 129
elevation, 13, 16–19, 48–52
El Niño, 56–58, 74, 163
Emanuel, Kerry, 164
emission, light and, 23
emissions reduction
    air pollution trends and, 124–126
    changing energy sources and, 127–129
    individuals and, 166–167
    politics and, 133–135
    power plants and, 129–130
    vehicles and, 130–133
energy, 8–9, 26–28, 68, 127–129, 132, 166
Energy Star program, 166
environment, evolution and, 16
Environmental Protection Agency (EPA), 126–127
equator, 27–28
evaporation, 8–9, 39
evaporative cooling, 39
evapotranspiration, 143
Evelyn, John, 89
evolution of atmosphere, 14–16

F

fog, 53–54, 113, 117
forests, 58, 87–88, 97, 114, 117–119. *See also* trees
fossil fuels
    acid rain and, 111–114
    air pollution and, 83–86
    alternatives to, 127–129
    carbon dioxide balance and, 5–7
    climate change and, 159, 170–171
freshwater ecosystems, 117
frogs, 117, 118

fronts, 47–48, 52
fuel cell technology, 131–133
Fumifugium (Evelyn), 89

G

gases, 3–7, 13–16, 18, 26
gasification, 129–130
geothermal energy, 127
Germany, 119
global warming. *See* climate change
greenhouse effect, 10, 14
greenhouse gases, 10–12, 84, 153, 158–161
Greenpeace, 119
ground cover, 140–141, 154–155
Gulf Stream, 39, 41
gyres, 40

H

Haagen-Smit, Arie, 90–91
Hadley cells, 31
hail, 52–53, 62
health
    asthma and, 105–106
    costs of air pollution and, 108–109
    deaths from air pollution and, 108
    effects of air pollution and, 102–104
    lung cancer and, 106–108
    metal poisoning and, 104–105
    ozone loss and, 150–152, 154
    people at risk from and, 101–102
heat, 8, 22–23, 38–39, 74–76, 158–159
heat index, 75–76
heat transfer, 17–18
hot spots, 135
humidity, 8

100-year storms, 67
hurricanes, 65, 68–74, 164
hybrid vehicles, 131
hydrocarbons, 11
hydrogen energy, 132–133
hydropower, 127

I

India, 65, 96–97, 120
individuals, 135–137, 166–168
Industrial Revolution, 12, 158
infrared energy, 18–19
infrared light, 8–9
insulation, 10
interglacial periods, 158
inversions, 20, 47, 93–96, 99, 163

J

jet streams, 33–34

K

Karnak, 120
Katrina (hurricane), 72–73
kinetic energy, 131
Künast, Renate, 119
Kyoto Protocol, 165

L

lakes, 117
land breezes, 54–55
La Niña, 57
latent heat, 38–39
latitude, 27–28, 30, 35–37
layers of atmosphere, 18–20
lead, 86, 103
light, overview of, 22–26
lightning, 60–61
lime, 116, 121
limestone buildings, 120–121
local winds, 54–56
London, 89–90
Los Angeles, 86, 90–91, 93, 95–96, 125
lung cancer, 106–108

M

measurements, air quality and, 126–127
melanoma, 151, 155
mercury, 85–86, 104–105, 135
metal poisoning, 104–105, 118
meteorology, 64
methane, 10, 12, 51, 88
Mexico City, 82, 108
microbursts, 62–63
mirages, 25–26
Molina, Mario, 148–149
Moller, Alan, 64
monsoons, 65, 163–164
Montreal Protocol, 147
motion, altitude, pressure, temperature and, 16–18
mountains, 41–42, 51–52, 54–55, 94

N

Nagin, Ray, 72–73
national parks, 94, 97–99
National Severe Storm Laboratory, 64
National Weather Service, 64
New Orleans, 72–73
nimbostratus clouds, 50
nimbus clouds, 48–49
nitrogen, 3–4, 14
nitrogen oxides (NOx)
    acid rain and, 111–114, 121
    cap-and-trade programs and, 134–135
    catalytic converters and, 130–131
    as greenhouse gases, 10, 84–85
    health and, 103
    as pollutant, 11
Nobel Prize, 148
noble gases, 4–5
noctilucent clouds, 51
Nor'easters, 67
nuclear power, 127

O

occluded fronts, 48
oceans, 37–41, 155–156
Ogden, Svante, 115
oxidation, 14–15
oxygen, 3–4, 5–7, 14
ozone
    atmospheric composition
        and, 7
    effects of on environment,
        96–97
    health and, 101–104, 106
    Los Angeles and, 95, 125
    national parks and, 98–99
    as secondary air pollutant,
        11, 83, 86–87
    in stratosphere, 147
ozone layer, defined, 7, 19, 20
ozone loss
    agriculture, health and, 154
    antarctic ozone hole and,
        149–152
    chlorofluorocarbons (CFCs)
        and, 148–149
    Montreal Protocol and, 147,
        152–153
    natural environment and,
        154–156

P

particulates
    biomass burning and, 87–88
    condensation and, 10–11
    effects of on environment,
        95–96
    health and, 103, 104, 106,
        108, 125
    heat islands and, 141–142
Peru Current, 56–57
petroleum, 83–84, 111–114
pH, 112. *See also* acid rain
Phoenix, AZ, 139–140, 141
photochemical smog, 11, 86–
    87, 90–91, 93–96, 125
photosynthesis, 5, 94–96

phytoplankton, 56–57, 84,
    155–156
Pinatubo, Mt., 24
polar front, 31–33
polar ice caps, 161
polar jet stream, 32
polar regions, 28
polar stratospheric clouds
    (PSCs), 51, 149
politics, 133–135
pollutants, defined, 3
pollution. *See* air pollution
ponds, 117
Pontchartrain, Lake, 73
population growth, 124
ports, 125
power plants, 129–130
precipitation, 9–11, 31, 52–53,
    68, 76–78
pressure, atmospheric, 16–18,
    28–30
Propper, Catherine, 95

R

radar, 64
radiation, 8–9, 27
radiation fog, 54
rainbows, 24–25
rain shadow effect, 41–42
reflection, 23, 26–27
refraction, 24–26
respiration, 5
rivers, 117
rotation, 29–30, 65–66, 68
Rowland, Sherwood, 148–149

S

Sacramento, CA, 141–143
Sacramento Shade, 142
Saffir-Simpson Hurricane
    Scale, 70, 164
Santa Ana winds, 55–56
satellites, 126–127
Scandinavia, 114–115, 119,
    152

scattering, 23, 26–27
scrubbers, 129
sea breezes, 54–55
sea surface temperatures,
    56–57, 162
Shenandoah National Park,
    97–99
shortwave radiation, 7–9, 20,
    150–152, 154–155
skin, 150–152
slash-and-burn agriculture, 87
Smith, Robert Angus, 115, 120
smog, 89–90. *See also* photo-
    chemical smog
snails, 118
snow, 52, 113
snow-blindness, 154
soil, 116, 118
solar energy, 26–27, 127
solar stoplight, 155
solar wind, 20
Sonora Desert, 139–140
specific heat, 39
spectrums, 25
speed, 30
squall lines, 60, 62
stationary fronts, 48
steam fog, 54
steam vents, 14
stomata, 96
storm chasers, 64
storm surge, 69
stratocumulus clouds, 50
stratosphere, 7, 20, 51. *See also*
    ozone loss
stratus clouds, 48–49, 50
subtropical jet stream, 33
sulfur dioxide
    acid rain and, 111–114,
        121
    asthma and, 106
    cap-and-trade programs
        and, 134–135
    health and, 103
    as pollutant, 11, 85

Sun, radiation and, 8–9
Sun Protection Factor (SPF), 151
sunset, 24
surge, 69
sustainability, 136
syngas, 129–130

T
Taj Mahal, 120
Tambora, Mt., 58
taxes, 167–168
temperature, 17–19, 138–140, 161–163
temperature inversions. *See* inversions
temples, 120
Thermodynamics, 132
thunderstorms, 59–63, 141
tidal surge, 67–68
topography, 93, 94
tornadoes, 63, 68
trade winds, 31, 40, 69, 74
transportation, 125, 130–133, 135–136, 166–167
trees, 97, 142, 154–155. *See also* forests
troposphere, 11, 18–20, 49, 153, 159–160
typhoons, 68

U
Union of Concerned Scientists, 166
upslope fog, 54

urban heat island effect, 138, 139–140, 141–143
Urban Heat Island Pilot Project (UHIPP), 141–142
UV radiation, 7–9, 20, 150–152, 154–155

V
valley breezes, 54–55
vegetation, 140–141, 154–155
vehicles, 125, 130–133, 135–136, 166–167
viruses, 107
visible light, 8–9
volatile organic compounds (VOCs), 81, 88–89, 130–131
volcanoes, 14, 58

W
Waldsterben, 119
warm fronts, 47–48
waste heat, 140
wastes, 11–12
water vapor, 7–9, 12
wavelengths, 8–9, 23
weather
    air masses and, 45–47
    climate change and, 162–163
    climate vs., 45
    clouds and, 48–52
    cyclones and, 65–68
    drought and, 76–78

El Niño and, 56–58
fog and, 53–54
forests and, 58
fronts and, 47–48
heat and, 74–76
hurricanes and, 68–74
jet streams and, 32–33
local winds and, 54–56
monsoons and, 65
precipitation and, 52–53
thunderstorms, tornadoes and, 59–64
tropospheric air movement and, 20
urban vs. rural, 138–141
volcanoes and, 58
westerly winds, 31, 40, 67
Westminster Abbey, 120
willi-willis, 68
wind, 20, 28–30, 54–56, 65, 68. *See also* trade winds; westerly winds
wind belts, 22, 30–33
windmills, 127
wind shear, 164

Y
Yellowstone National Park, 99

Z
zooplankton, 84

About the Author

DANA DESONIE, PH.D., has written about the earth, ocean, space, life, and environmental sciences for more than a decade. Her work has appeared in educational lessons, textbooks, and magazines, and on radio and the Web. Her 1996 book, *Cosmic Collisions*, described the importance of asteroids and comets in Earth history and the possible consequences of a future asteroid collision with the planet. Before becoming a science writer, she received a doctorate in oceanography, spending weeks at a time at sea, mostly in the tropics, and one amazing day at the bottom of the Pacific in the research submersible *Alvin*. She now resides in Phoenix, Arizona, with her neuroscientist husband, Miles Orchinik, and their two children.